A FAITH TO MEET OUR FEARS

A FAITH TO MEET OUR FEARS

Charles B. Bugg

PEAKE ROAD

Macon, Georgia

ISBN 1-57312-093-6

A Faith to Meet Our Fears

Charles B. Bugg

Copyright © 1997

Peake Road
6316 Peake Road
Macon, Georgia 31210-3960
1-800-747-3016

Biblical quotations, unless otherwise noted, are from the
New Revised Standard Version of the Bible (NRSV).

The paper used in this publication
meets the minimum requirements of
American National Standard for Information Sciences—
Permanence of Paper for Printed Library Materials.
ANSI Z39.48–1984

Library of Congress Cataloging-in-Publication

Bugg, Charles B.
    A faith to meet our fears / Charles B. Bugg.
    xii + 84pp.   6" x 9" (15 x 23cm.)
    ISBN 1-57312-093-6   (alk. paper)
    1. Baptists—Sermons. 2. Sermons, American. I. Title.
    BX6333.B84F25   1997
    252'.061—dc20   97-38537
                                                                     CIP

TO MY DAD
Whose gifts of love and listening have been a constant source of strength.

Contents

Foreword

Robert Frost once confided that "all poetry begins as a lump in the throat." The words that have found their home inside the walls of this book must have come from somewhere in that same vicinity. They carry with them the quiet power and unvarnished honesty of words that must have gotten their start as "a lump in the throat" of this gifted writer, preacher, professor, and minister, Charles Bugg.

Dr. Bugg's words seem to travel to somewhere deep within our own pain and joy because they seem to emerge from somewhere deep inside his own pain and joy. On these pages, "deep calls to deep," as the writer's words travel from the depth of who he is to the depth of who we are. What must have started out as a lump in Chuck Bugg's throat, becomes help and hope for you and me—not maudlin, starry-eyed help and hope, but genuine, clear-eyed help and hope that is undergirded by honest, livable biblical theology.

To recast the line from Frost, "All good preaching begins as a lump in the throat." From somewhere in that vicinity, the words that wait inside these walls have found their way to your eyes and mine. They will speak to the lump in our throat and to the pain in our lives, and they will point us in the direction of strength and hope . . . the kind of strength and hope that really matters in our kind of world.

Charles E. Poole
First Baptist Church
Washington, D.C.

Acknowledgments

Cicero said, "Gratitude is the parent of all virtues." The Bible doesn't say it exactly the same way, but it certainly stresses the power of gratitude. On the last night of his earthly life, what did Jesus do? He took the occasion of a simple meal with his disciples and gave thanks for what he had. I wonder how I would have responded given the same set of circumstances? I want to take this opportunity to say thanks to some people, and my prayer is that my saying thanks arises out of a life that is becoming more thankful.

I am grateful for the people across the years who have listened to my sermons. They have given me the gift of their attention. What a gift! I think of the folks at Providence Baptist Church in Charlotte, North Carolina, who have given ears to the sound of my voice as together we have sought God's face each Sunday. These people have cared for my family and me and have encouraged me beyond what I deserve.

I'm thankful for my administrative assistant, Linda Burris. Not only has she endured my scratchy handwriting, but also she has told me how much the sermons have meant to her. Those of us who preach know how much this means, especially when we put our words into writing. I always feel I could and should have done better.

I am especially grateful for Diane. We married twenty-eight years ago. I became her husband and by default her preacher. She sees me Monday through Saturdays. Diane knows my limits better than anyone else. My wife knows that if a minister has to embody the fruit of the Spirit all through the week in order to climb into the pulpit, I would be disqualified on most Sundays. Yet, Diane has been my best friend and the best fan of my preaching. She thinks I'm the best, and I certainly am not going to try to change her mind.

I have so much for which to be thankful. I am trying more to give thanks and to live thanks.

Chapter 1
Do We Have to Be Perfect?

Come to me, all you that are weary and are carrying heavy burdens, and I will give you rest. Take my yoke upon you, and learn from me; for I am gentle and humble in heart, and you will find rest for your souls. For my yoke is easy, and my burden is light. (Matt 11: 28-30)

I have a brother who is a trial attorney. He spends most of his time defending people or companies he represents. Suppose today I took my brother's place and became the attorney. I'm here to defend "perfectionism." I believe I can make a good case for it.

Most of us grew up with the admonition, "Do your best," ringing in our ears. We went to school and learned that the "A" students were the ones who were usually noticed by the teachers. In fact, it was even better if you made 100 percent. Some of us learned our lesson well. Anything less than absolute perfection was not acceptable.

When we finished school, we went off to live life that way. We were going to be perfect spouses, perfect parents, perfect ministers, perfect accountants, perfect homemakers, perfect in everything. Deep down we knew we weren't perfect. In fact, we criticized ourselves unmercifully for every mistake. We lived with constant anxiety. Our doing and being became meshed. When we did something wrong, we were all wrong as persons. We didn't tolerate others' shortcomings very well either because it reminded us we weren't perfect.

Our daughter was born when I was a seminary student. One of my good friends had a child born about the same time. Would you believe his daughter was walking well before Laura Beth? My child crawled well, but she didn't walk. For me it was competition. I was losing the race for the "perfect" child.

Of course, I can make a good case for perfectionism. What if we turned the world over to people who were just content to get by with the minimum and who weren't bothered by mistakes. Our world is impressed by "shakers and movers." We like "self-starters." Who wants to hire somebody for a job when the applicant's first questions are, "Do you have pencils with big erasers?" and "How long is the lunch break?"

I can make a case for perfectionism. If I were an attorney, I would say, "What would the world be like if we didn't have perfectionists?" I can also make a case against it. Are you a perfectionist? Then you know the downside. For those of us who have perfectionistic tendencies, we know the anxiety, the anger and the self-depreciation that come with the territory. Spiritually, we hear the call of Jesus to "do" something far more clearly than the call to "be" something. Grace is a concept. Works is the reality by which we live.

That's why I have always been so fascinated by these words of Jesus. They were spoken in the midst of his ministry to an audience identified simply as the "crowd" (v. 7). Jesus wasn't speaking to a convention of perfectionists, but He could have been. These words have a soft sound. They're inviting, intimate words.

COME . . .

Jesus said first, "Come to me, all you that are weary and carrying heavy burdens." When I taught preaching at Southern Baptist Theological Seminary, I developed a strong interest in the relationship between proclamation and the preacher's own spiritual formation. Most of the homiletical books I read dealt with preaching as a "craft." Attention focused on issues such as the structure and delivery of the sermon. The formation of the sermon was the focus. What concerned me was the lack of attention to the formation of the one who preached. After all, a sermon is never separated from its spokesperson. We hear not just preaching, but a "person preaching."

By nature, I'm not a particularly pious person who spends long periods in prayer. I like activity. I measure myself by my "doing." So I wanted to test my theory about the importance of spiritual formation. I signed up for a prayer retreat in which much of the time was unstructured. I remember how hard that was for me, especially at first. Frankly, it seemed like a waste trying to find God in the trees, the pine cones, and the cloud formations. I kept thinking about the people back in the real world who probably needed my presence.

Yet, one thing the leader of the retreat had said at the beginning kept gnawing at me. "What is your own image of God?" he asked. "Not what do you tell people about God as a preacher, but what is your own functional image of God?" "Think," the leader had said, "about how you see God. That will tell you much about how you pray or don't pray."

I have not forgotten that question. I'm not speaking so much about the shape of God. Who knows that? I'm not talking about philosophy of religion where we debate God as the "First Cause" or the "Unmoved Mover." I'm really thinking about a more primal level. For example, can God be trusted with my life? Can I rest in God? Is God always calling me to do something, or can I simply be and receive?

"Come . . . all," Jesus said. All—winners, losers, successes, failures, good, bad—all! Come! It's an admonition, but it's gentle and filled with grace. Eugene Peterson has a wonderful phrase: the "unforced rhythm of grace." Perfectionistic people keep trying to force things. We force ourselves and those around us to live up to impossible expectations. Those days of retreat as I pondered trees and pine cones, I really thought about my image of God. Do I trust God? Can I come to God and simply "be" loved by God for who I am and not what I do? Will I ever learn to be and to receive the unforced rhythm of grace?

TAKE . . .

Jesus gave a second admonition that day, "Take my yoke upon you." Jesus' first-century hearers would have been familiar with his image of a yoke. A yoke was a harness or collar that fit over the neck and shoulders of an animal. The owner of the animal used the yoke to guide the animal as the owner wanted.

What do perfectionistic people often experience? Anxiety? Why? Well, when you set impossible expectations, you can't meet them.

The amount of anxiety we feel is usually the distance between what we expect of ourselves and what we achieve.

Jesus said, "Take my yoke upon you." In other words, let me guide and direct your life. Then Jesus made a remarkable comment: "For my yoke is easy, and my burden is light." Perfectionistic preachers seldom talk about these words. We are into challenge and costly discipleship. Invite us for a revival because we preach the demands of Jesus and call the church to be more. When we preach, we can leave everybody anxious.

Of course, Jesus' preaching does have demand. He calls us to follow him, which is no small task. But Jesus' preaching is also filled with compassion, care, and acceptance. We are called not to worry. We are told to trust in a God who comes as gift and grace. We are asked to take his yoke, and then Jesus says, "For my yoke is easy, and my burden is light."

Not long ago, I took a trip out of town with my wife. We had three days together, just the two of us. We left our son, the chair of the deacons, the head of the finance committee, and the church staff. In other words, the idea was to get away. However, I did take the briefcase. I took several books I wanted to read, sermons to work on, and some writing I wanted to do. By the second day, my wife was laughing. I wasn't. I was already behind what I had expected to do. "Why didn't you leave the briefcase back home along with the chair of deacons?" she asked. Diane doesn't understand. I feel undressed without my briefcase. I also felt very anxious with it and everything I had crammed into it.

LEARN . . .

"Come," Jesus said, "take my yoke," and then Jesus gave one more admonition. "Learn from me," he said, "for I am gentle and humble in heart, and you will find rest for your souls." Jesus was a masterful teacher. His images are unforgettable. The disciples, the crowd, even Jesus' enemies all seemed to agree that he had the gift to teach. Even without formal education, Jesus had people such as the well-trained Nicodemus say, "We know that you are a rabbi come from God." Jesus taught with words.

He also taught by example. "Learn from me; for I am gentle and humble in heart, and you will find rest for your souls." Rest. That

he vocabulary of people driven by perfectionism. Do
I really believe? Some of us begin to think we are
the work of the Kingdom. That's why I always carry
ase with too much to do. After all, who's going to
dom if I'm not well read and well prepared. There's
hint of egotism. How can you rest or be gentle or
rything is on your shoulders?

slightly morbid, but it has a point. When I went to
Seminary, I was surprised to learn that one of the
as a family burial plot in the nearby Cave Hill
right. Seminary teaching didn't pay all that well to
things would be taken care of when I died.
st that benefit when I left the faculty.

ould tell my preaching classes about my space at
sured the students I hadn't come to the seminary
cemetery. But each time I drove by Cave Hill, it
my mortality and the fact that the Kingdom of
ithout me or my briefcase. I had a few students
they were indispensable and had come to the
time as this. I wanted them to know that a great
ow that we depend on God, and that God is not
nearly as anxious as we that everything is just right.

It's true. I can make a case for perfectionism. I've spent much of
my life making that case. The fact is I really don't want to keep
doing life that way. It's too tiring. I don't like the constant anxiety. I
don't like being angry with everyone around me who doesn't get it
all right. I want to change. "Come, take, and learn from me," Jesus
said. I'm ready to listen. Are you?

Chapter 2
When Anger Gets the Best of Us

But this was very displeasing to Jonah, and he became angry. He prayed to the Lord and said, "O Lord! Is not this what I said when I was still in my own country? That is why I fled to Tarshish at the beginning; for I knew that you are a gracious God and merciful, slow to anger, and abounding in steadfast love, and ready to relent from punishing. And now, O Lord, please take my life from me, for it is better for me to die than to live." And the Lord said, "Is it right for you to be angry?" Then Jonah went out of the city and sat down east of the city, and made a booth for himself there. He sat under it in the shade, waiting to see what would become of the city.

The Lord God appointed a bush, and made it come up over Jonah, to give shade over his head, to save him from his discomfort; so Jonah was very happy about the bush. But when dawn came up the next day, God appointed a worm that attacked the bush, so that it withered. When the sun rose, God prepared a sultry east wind, and the sun beat down on the head of Jonah so that he was faint and asked that he might die. He said, "It is better for me to die than to live."

But God said to Jonah, "Is it right for you to be angry about the bush?" And he said, "Yes, angry enough to die." Then the Lord said, "You are concerned about the bush, for which you did not labor and which you did not grow; it came into being in a night and perished in a night. And should I not be concerned about Nineveh, that great city, in which there are more than a hundred and twenty thousand persons who do not know their right hand from their left, and also many animals?"
(Jonah 4:1-11)

On August 12, 1994, the *USA Today* newspaper reported an incident aboard a Korean airlines jet. The pilot and co-pilot got into an argument about whether there was enough runway to land the airplane. Both of them struggled for the controls. When the plane finally landed, it skidded and rammed a safety barrier. Fortunately, the 152 passengers and eight crew members escaped before the plane burst into flames.

I have always assumed that the crew members on airplanes on which I fly have a good or at least a cordial relationship. Frankly, I never thought about anger in the cockpit. Now, when I board an airplane, I look to the left to see if everybody at the controls looks fairly happy. I'm grateful the incident in Korea ended safely for the passengers. However, I would prefer those at the controls handle their hostilities differently.

Let's face it, though. Anger is a part of the fabric of human life. It's a feeling. Some of us have been taught to suppress it. "Don't get angry," we've been told, which really means "don't show your anger." Keep it inside, keep it to yourself, keep on smiling. The fact is Jesus became angry on occasions and showed it. The book of James reads, "Be angry and sin not." Yet, growing up in the church, I got the impression the Bible was saying, "Be angry and it's a sin."

The biblical text is from Jonah. I've chosen these words because it's a picture of a person who is angry. God calls Jonah to preach to the people of Nineveh, the capital of Assyria. This is not a happy assignment for the prophet. Jonah tells God that he really wants to preach in Tarshish. After all, the Assyrians had conquered and humiliated Israel. Jonah despised what they had done to his people. Why would the God of Abraham, Isaac, and Jacob want the Assyrians to get in on the good news of God's presence? "I'll go to Tarshish," Jonah says.

After a series of misadventures, including time in the great fish's belly, Jonah lands in Nineveh. Reluctantly, he calls the people to repentance. Jonah's hoping the Ninevites won't listen. However, the most amazing thing happens. For three days Jonah preaches, and everybody—including the king—responds and repents. This is even better than a Billy Graham crusade. Everybody in Nineveh comes to God, and God has compassion and forgives them.

Why this is a preacher's deepest dream! Can you imagine some Sunday when you have a headache and your heart's not in it? You would rather be home in bed. You're not even sure you like the congregation, and you wish God would send you to Tarshish or Timbuktu. You make it to the church house, you preach, and on that day everybody—I mean *everybody*—gets right with God.

I would be ecstatic. Funny thing, though, Jonah is angry. "I knew," Jonah cries out, "that you are a gracious God and merciful, slow to anger and abounding in steadfast love, and ready to relent from punishing." In other words, God does exactly what Jonah does not want. Jonah hates the Ninevites; he is angry with them, and the God who is "slow to anger" thrusts out the boundaries of God's love and saves the enemy.

What Makes Us Angry?

One of the issues this story raises is the question, "What makes us angry?" What made Jonah angry? He saw the Assyrians as enemies. God saw the Assyrians as persons. That's one issue. But another issue is that in this situation Jonah didn't have control. Jonah didn't get his way. The prophet had his expectations of what was right and fair. What he wanted, however, didn't happen. He became angry.

Several years ago, I took my family on a trip to Miami, Florida. That's my hometown. I wanted to take my wife and children to all the places that held memory for me: the old church, the old school, the old ballfield, the field of my dreams. When I was about nine years old, I would gather with a group of friends for a "pick-up" game. We had no umpires. We played and called the game ourselves, and that was the problem. Invariably, a disagreement broke out. Everybody took sides, and whoever brought the bat and ball said if it's not done my way, I'm going home. I never remember completing a game.

Maybe we can excuse that behavior for nine-year-olds, but if we're thirty-nine or fifty-nine and still saying, it's my way or no way, we have a problem. Let's be fair to Jonah. He had some good reasons to be angry with the Assyrians. That was a tough crowd. If I were asked to preach, I would have chosen Tarshish. Jonah had a point.

But isn't that the point. When I get angry, I usually feel justified. "I wasn't treated fairly," I will say, and maybe I wasn't. I didn't get the promotion, the recognition, the approval or whatever I'm looking for, and perhaps I did deserve it. I mean, humanly speaking, did Nineveh deserve the grace of God? And, of course, who of us ever does?

We need to be careful. Some things deserve our anger. Forty thousand people a day in our world die of hunger, and I'm scraping food off my plate. Little children killed on urban streets, drug-infested neighborhoods, families deserted by fathers and husbands, pornography that turns persons into objects, the increasing violence on television and in movies, churches that get turned in on themselves—you could add to the list or make your own. Some things should make us angry, so angry that we do something about them.

Yet, some things are beyond our control. These were people in Nineveh. Let's not forget that. To Jonah they may have been just Assyrians, and Jonah believed the only good Assyrian was a dead one. It's easy to dismiss people by putting a label on them. Black/white, male/female, liberal/conservative . . . why, we can take shots at people and not feel a thing if we can categorize them. The fact is Jonah didn't get his way, and he was angry.

I remember well the months following our ten year old son's diagnosis. Diane and I stood in the hospital, and all it took was one sentence from the doctor, "Your son has a malignant brain tumor." The physician may have said, "I'm sorry," or something else, but I was frozen in time by "malignant brain tumor." In the days following, numbness turned into grief that turned into anger. If I ever knew in my life that I wasn't in control, it was then; and it was painful. In moments like that you try to change what you can. As David's parents, Diane and I did all we could to get him the best medical resources. Yet, there was so much that couldn't be changed —that somehow had to be lived with, that had to be accepted.

Is that also a miracle? Acceptance? I always thought miracles were when something changed. You don't like Nineveh. You tell God. God says, "If it's Tarshish you want, Tarshish you will have?" And Jonah lived happily ever after. Would that have been a miracle? Or is the miracle that in the tough place we ourselves may come to know that God is in control, and we are changed? Jonah is a sad story. Through his preaching, the congregation is converted. The one who is not converted is the preacher. "It's my way or no way," Jonah says. That's sad. Jonah loses. He can't rejoice in the conversion of persons, and he can't rejoice in the compassion of God.

How Do We Handle Our Anger?

How does Jonah handle this anger? God comes to Jonah after the city has been converted, and God says, "Is it right for you to be angry?" (v. 4). What does Jonah say? Nothing! He goes to a place east of the city, finds some shade, and sits there to see what will happen in Nineveh. Undoubtedly, Jonah hoped that the Ninevites' new religion wouldn't stick, and they would be back quickly to the old ways. What impresses me, however, is that Jonah never responds to God's question. It's called the silent treatment.

Conflict arises in a marriage, and the next sound is the bedroom door slamming. "Can't we talk about it?" Silence. Or the business meeting at the church? We need new carpet. My group wants red. The other group wants blue. The vote is taken. It's blue, and the next sound is the sanctuary door slamming. "It's our way or no way," one of the reds says. Can't we talk about it? Why do we always turn things into win/lose situations? Why do we put ourselves into something so that if it's not done our way, we see it as a rejection of ourselves? Jonah didn't get his way. He turned the whole thing into a contest of wills. "Is it right for you to be angry?" God asks. No response. The pouting prophet heads to the east side of Nineveh to sit and wait.

While Jonah is waiting, a vine grows up to give him shade. Then a worm eats the vine, and Jonah sits in the scorching sun. "It is better for me to die than to live," Jonah concludes. God then asks, "Is it right for you to be angry about the bush?" "Yes," Jonah replied. "[I am] angry enough to die." Give Jonah some credit. At least now he's talking. He's even making some sense. Wouldn't we be upset if our shade was disturbed, our comfort challenged?

Yet, Jonah still didn't get the point. Who made the vine? Who made the Ninevites? Who made you, Jonah? The fact is it's all a gift, a gift from God. We take it for granted. We even begin to believe that vines, people, and even ourselves are our possession. We are in control. We take charge. When the vine wilts, Jonah is ready to die because life after all should work his way.

But it doesn't always, does it? Sometimes life really doesn't work according to our dreams. What do we do, then? Spend the rest of our days in rage? Jonah didn't get it. The vine is God's; the Ninevites are God's; Jonah is God's; life is God's. As far as we know, the Ninevites were changed. Jonah never was. He never saw whatever was as the gift of God's grace.

I want to live with more grace and gratitude. Don't you? I'm tired of anger that does nothing except corrode my spirit. I'm tired of thinking that life must happen as I believe best. I want to see myself, you, and even events I don't understand as somehow parts of God's grace. In a word, I want to see all of life as a gift.

Chapter 3
The Faith That Matters

But if I go to the east, he is not there; if I go to the west, I do not find him. When he is at work in the north, I do not see him; when he turns to the south, I catch no glimpse of him. But he knows the way that I take; when he has tested me, I will come forth as gold. (Job 23:8-10 NIV)

One of the most popular movies in recent years was *Forrest Gump*. Tom Hanks plays a young man with an I.Q. of 75. The movie traces Forrest's life through a series of events. It quickly becomes apparent that Forrest is especially close to his mother. In fact, Forrest relies heavily on the wise advice his mother gives him.

When people call him stupid, Forrest remembers his mother's words: "Stupid is as stupid does." "Everybody has a destiny," Forrest contends, recalling the conviction of his mother. Then there is the most memorable line of the movie: "Life is like a box of chocolates. You never know which one you will get." "Mama," Forrest observes, "could always say things in ways that I could understand."

These words from the story in the book of Job are said in ways we can understand. Job is trying to fathom the fact of his own suffering. He is especially wondering, "Where is God?" In his mind Job travels to the far corners of the world, and he returns from his mental journey with no glimpse of God. East, West, North, South—Job tries to find the divine in each direction, and Job's conclusion is that God is nowhere to be found.

Yet, the final word is not despair. "But," Job says more by faith than by sight, "God knows the way that I take; when God has tested me, I will come forth as gold." "Mama could always say things in ways that I could understand," Forrest recalled, and that is also the power of this biblical text. Job faced enormous losses in his life. The grief he felt was unmeasurable. He struggled to find a sense of God, and Job's description is profound and powerful.

The Facts of the Matter

One thing that makes this passage of Scripture so powerful is that it honestly portrays the facts of the matter. The Bible deals with life as it is, not as we may wish it to be. Not only has Job lost family, health, and possessions; he has lost God. "I have looked everywhere," Job is saying, "for some sign of God and nothing!" Job is alone with his anguish; he has grief but no God.

For Father's Day one year, my daughter gave me a special gift. In a frame she put a picture of me with her when she was a little girl, and around the picture she had written special memories. I felt like crying and laughing at the same time. She recalled her baptism, learning to drive, going to college, getting married, a favorite Bible verse we shared together whenever she faced a tough time. There were other things she wrote that brought back a flood of memories for me.

I suppose I wanted to cry because all of those things reminded me of the baby that had become a child and the child that is now a young woman. Life seems to have moved so fast. One day she was her Daddy's girl, and before I knew it I was performing her wedding and "giving her away" to her husband. Actually, I didn't "give" her away. I paid lots of money to become the number-two man in my daughter's life, which may have been another reason for my tears.

Just in the ordinary events of life we experience grief and loss. Can you imagine how Job must have felt? Virtually everything he loved had been lost, and even his wife and so-called friends were no help. "Why don't you curse God?" his wife counseled. His friends turned philosophical. According to them, Job's problems must have been caused by his sin or the fact that God, if there was one, didn't really care what happened to him. One of his friends said, "Don't question what has happened"—which is difficult when your whole world has been shaken.

"Mama," Forrest Gump boasted, "could always say things in ways that I could understand." What about God? There are times in all of our lives when we yearn to understand or at least to catch a glimpse of God in our grief. East, West, North, South—in every direction Job casts his eyes, and he sees nothing resembling God. "I catch no glimpse of Him," Job says—not even a glimpse of God, much less a full view of God's will and how God may be using Job's pain to achieve some purpose.

I have called this section "the facts of the matter" because the fact of the matter is that on any given Sunday those of us who preach are speaking to people who feel God's absence. For some reason they have come to the meeting place. Maybe it is to escape the loneliness that is often the companion of loss. Maybe it is the hope that through a word or a song or a smile or a hug they may catch a glimpse of God. Or maybe it is to hear from preachers like us who share the word that we, too, understand the absence of God. Courage comes when we know that we aren't the only ones who have wanted to see God, only to stare into what seems like a black hole.

I'm not talking about the kind of preaching that has no word of assurance. Neither am I suggesting that the pulpit be turned into a place where only doubt and despair are dispensed. But I am talking about understanding. I'm speaking about the honesty of the Bible where a man named Job goes searching for God and returns without even a glimpse.

When I have taught preaching, I have also served as interim minister at several churches. I learned my place as an interim pastor one Sunday when I was standing at the door after the morning service. A little boy told me he liked me, but then he said, "I will be glad when we get a real pastor." As an interim I found myself living with a congregation through the grief of a minister who had gone and the anxiety about whoever might come.

Their pastor was gone—an experience of grief. Even if some in the congregation were happy to see the former pastor gone, it was still a loss. The church was living in the "in-between time." As the little boy said, I was there until the church could get someone "real." Things were changing; the church prayed for leadership; the pastor search committee went East, West, North, and South and sometimes returned without a glimpse of God. I stood each Sunday to preach between the pillars of grief and anxiety.

The Bible is real even if some of us who preach are tempted at times not to be. It does not traffic in easy answers or deny that life is demanding and difficult. Job goes looking for God, and when he returns he confesses, "I catch no glimpse of Him." The fact of the matter is God is not to be found.

The Faith That Matters

Yet, it is here that the text takes a striking turn, and Job takes a leap of faith. Reading Job's story, you might expect he would continue down the road of despair. After all, Job looked for God but didn't see God. You might think that Job would become curdled with cynicism. If I can't see God, I might conclude that there is no God or that God simply doesn't care.

Listen though to Job's response: "But God knows the way that I take; when God has tested me, I will come forth as gold." The facts of the matter are God can't be found in any direction. The faith that matters, however, is Job's conviction that God is still directing his life. "But God knows. . . ." What a remarkable statement of faith!

The novelist Ernest Hemingway used to say that all of us are broken, but some of us become strong at the broken places. You may remember that Hemingway could not tolerate his own brokenness, and one day ended his life. But, in my opinion, there is remarkable truth in Hemingway's observation about life. All of us are broken. Granted, we don't all suffer losses like Job. Granted, the way seems easier for some. Yet, in one way or another, all of us are acquainted with grief.

Do we get stronger at the broken places? Not necessarily. Some become obsessed with their brokenness. Some spend all of their days and nights trying to understand why it happened to them. Some try to find God and conclude—at least for all practical purposes—God is dead.

It would have been easy for Job to take any of these directions. The man was hurting; his search to see God was fruitless. But how does he respond. It's here that Job moves beyond the level of what can be seen and known and understood to the level of faith. "But God knows," and that becomes the power to move on. Was it easy for Job? I doubt it. Real faith never is easy because it takes suffering and sadness seriously. It doesn't pretend that we live in the best of all possible worlds. Real faith recognizes injustice but then amazingly affirms, "God knows."

"Mama could always say things in ways that I could understand," Forrest Gump said. You have to envy someone who has a mother with an answer for every question. Sometimes I wish God would just say everything in ways I could understand. It would certainly make my preaching on Sundays much tighter and cleaner. That's not the way it is, though. On many Sundays I come to the pulpit. I know the pain of some, and I know my own pain. I don't have all the answers. Then I say, "But God knows." Now who believes that? And if we do, it makes all the difference.

In 1983, soon after our ten-year-old son was diagnosed with a malignant brain tumor, I came to preach one Sunday. I honestly wondered how I would make it through the sermon. I was tired, worried, struggling to make sense of what seemed to me senseless.

That Sunday our minister of music announced our first congregational hymn, "Great Is Thy Faithfulness." As we sang this hymn I knew by heart, I suddenly found my heart strangely touched. The first stanza became grace for me that day:

> Great is Thy faithfulness, O God my Father,
> There is no shadow of turning with Thee:
> Thou changest not, Thy compassions they fail not;
> As Thou hast been Thou forever wilt be.
>
> Great is Thy Faithfulness! Great is Thy Faithfulness!
> Morning by morning new mercies I see;
> All I have needed, Thy hand hath provided;
> Great is Thy Faithfulness, Lord unto me!

The fact is I could not sing those words by myself that day. My own faith was not that strong. I could only sing lifted up by the community of faith around me. I had looked in every direction I knew and had caught no glimpse of the divine. But the faith, the real faith that mattered was not in myself but in the God whose faithfulness is sure. Life changes. At times the shadows are thick. What do we do? Job said, "But God knows." The hymn writer said, "Great Is Thy Faithfulness."

Chapter 4
Listening for the Whisper

Now Ahab told Jezebel everything Elijah had done and how he had killed all the prophets with the sword. So Jezebel sent a messenger to Elijah to say, "May the gods deal with me, be it ever so severely, if by this time tomorrow I do not make your life like one of them." Elijah was afraid and ran for his life. When he came to Beersheba in Judah, he left his servant there, while he himself went a day's journey into the desert. He came to a broom tree, sat down under it and prayed that he might die. "I have had enough, Lord," he said. "Take my life; I am no better than my ancestors." Then he lay down under the tree and fell asleep. . . .

There he went into a cave and spent the night. And the word of the Lord came to him: "What are you doing here, Elijah?" He replied, "I have been very zealous for the Lord God Almighty. The Israelites have rejected your covenant, broken down your altars, and put your prophets to death with the sword. I am the only one left, and now they are trying to kill me too." The Lord said, "Go out and stand on the mountain in the presence of the Lord, for the Lord is about to pass by." Then a great and powerful wind tore the mountains apart and shattered the rocks before the Lord, but the Lord was not in the wind. After the wind there was an earthquake, but the Lord was not in the earthquake. After the earthquake came a fire, but the Lord was not in the fire. And after the fire came a gentle whisper. When Elijah heard it, he pulled his cloak over his face and went out and stood at the mouth of the cave. Then a voice said to him, "What are you doing here, Elijah?" (1 Kgs 19:1-5, 9-13 NIV)

I t had been a bad day at work for the father. When he walked into the house that evening, he said to his wife, "This has been a terrible day. Everything has gone wrong. Please, I don't want to hear any more bad news." "In that case," his wife replied, "you'll be happy to know that three out of your four children didn't break their arms today."

Most of us have experienced days like that. If it could go wrong, it did. Things piled up on us. We felt overwhelmed. The problems seemed so big, and we seemed so small in the face of them.

This was the story of Elijah. He had been to the top of Mount Carmel, and there he had done battle with the prophets of Baal. It seemed the best of times for Elijah. The 450 priests of Baal had called on their god to show himself, and nothing happened. No rain, no fire, no sign of their god. Elijah, the solitary prophet, called on his God, and the fire of the Lord fell. Elijah was a success. His God had won, and Elijah had carried the day.

But not everyone was happy. Jezebel, the queen, the wife of King Ahab, had brought her worship of Baal to Israel, and she was incensed at Elijah's triumph. The word hit the streets. Jezebel wanted Elijah dead. What do you think Elijah did? Do you think he stood in the middle of Main Street and shouted, "Bring Jezebel on"? Do you think Elijah knocked on the palace door and challenged the queen to a showdown in the state room? No, the brave prophet of Carmel ran for his life. He was afraid, overwhelmed. "Take my life, Lord," Elijah cried as he raced to a faraway cave.

Why the sudden change in Elijah? Was he tired? Successes can drain us. Fatigue makes us vulnerable. Did he expect that after Carmel all would go well? Successes can make us think that everything in life should go so well. Nothing irritates us more than the pestering person who won't let us revel in our victories. Or, maybe, there was something about Jezebel that brought out the worst in Elijah. Let's face it. Some people we meet affect us like fingernails on the chalkboard. Put them in a room with us and we tense up, get a headache, our stomachs twist and turn.

Whatever the reason, Elijah, who bravely faced trouble one moment, did an about-face the next and wanted to die. What would you call this? I would call it depression. Running away, by himself in the cave, self-confidence gone, wanting God to take his life. I would call it despair. The nineteenth chapter of 1 Kings is clear.

Losing . . . Faith in God

Elijah had lost his faith in God. Notice the difference in the way the prophet prayed. On Mount Carmel he had said, "O Lord, God of Abraham, Isaac and Israel, let it be known today that you are God in Israel and that I am your servant" (18:36a). But in the desert of despair under the broom tree, the prayer was different: "I have had enough, Lord. . . . Take my life; I am no better than my ancestors" (19:4b).

What a difference! One day Elijah seemed certain of who God was and certain he was God's servant. The next day he seemed certain of nothing except it was time to die. What changed? He hadn't become an atheist or agnostic. Elijah still prayed and still called God, "Lord," but there's a profound difference in the tone of the prayers.

"Listen to your children praying," the Negro spiritual says. Listen to us as we pray, and you can tell much about where we are, and what we are, and how we see who we are. It certainly is true in my belief. Belief in the existence of God is not the issue I face. Rather, it is trust in this God to provide, to be there for me and with me.

Jesus never invited anybody to believe that somewhere there was a God. Rather, Jesus invited people to a more daring adventure. "Follow me," he said to a group by the Sea of Galilee one day, and they probably never imagined how their lives would change. These disciples were given no directions except to follow. They were given no destination except to follow "me" wherever that road would lead.

It was a grand adventure in trust and faith. These men left their nets to follow the Nazarene. They left security for somebody who had come to save his people from their sins. Following God is risky business. If all we were called to do was to believe that God existed, that would be easy. Either God does or God doesn't; take your choice. But we are called to a life of trust. "Follow me," the stranger said one day, and the rest of the disciples' days were never the same.

Elijah is an easy target for those of us who preach. "Why did he run?" we ask. The answer is probably the same reason we want to run at times. Life is difficult. Problems abound. About the time we have it together, a Jezebel appears, and life begins to fall apart. Is God real in those moments? Can we trust God?

Several years ago, I was in the car with my daughter who was then a teenager. Since I was driving, I chose the radio station. That was the rule in our family. Whoever drove picked the music. It was one of those stations that played the "golden oldies." The song "I Believe" came on. In case you've forgotten some of the less than memorable lyrics, the song says, "I believe for every drop of rain that falls a flower grows; I believe in the darkest night a candle glows." I was so excited. "Laura Beth," I said, "That was my high school class song. Miami Senior High School, class of '61. I remember when we voted that as "our song."

"You're kidding, Dad. Your whole class voted that as your song. The words are sappy," my daughter said. I think she was jealous because at least you could understand the words. But she was right in one respect. If all we believe is that somewhere in the darkest night a candle glows, that is not much on which to build our lives. It hardly will get us through the valleys or by the Jezebels. The call to faith is deeper, riskier, stronger. Elijah seemed to have lost his faith or at least his faith in a God big enough for the days and nights of his life.

Losing . . . Faith in Ourselves

Elijah also lost his faith in himself. He told God to take his life, and then he said, "I am no better than my ancestors." Apparently, Elijah didn't have a high view of his forebears. They were dead; he should be dead, too. How did Elijah come to a place where he thought he would be better off dead than alive?

Could it be that he overexpected of life? What do you and I expect? How we answer that largely determines how we feel about life. After the exhilaration of Mount Carmel, Elijah may have concluded that this is the way life is. We go from one grand success to another. The applause of the crowd. The approval of those who watched. Elijah was the hero. All was going well. The prophet seemed to have the Midas touch. Then came Jezebel, and the party was over.

Some of us feed on approval and applause. We love it when things go well and people like what we're doing. We begin to imagine that this is what life should be. We should move from one success to the next. We expect things to be that way. And then comes the word of criticism from someone or the reality sinks in that we sometimes fail, and we begin to question our own worth.

Some religion feeds this idea. Triumphalist theology abounds these days. Everybody succeeds. Everybody gets rich. Everybody is made well. All of this is blessed in the name of God. There is no talk of failure. There is much made about the resurrection but little if anything said about crosses, graves, and death. Every day is Easter Sunday. The only problem is that this theology skips Good Friday.

How do we handle our own failures? Nobody I know gets married expecting to get divorced, but it happens. Nobody takes a job expecting to be fired, but it happens. Nobody I know wants to be afraid, but we are. Maybe Elijah thought that after Mount Carmel this is the way life should be: victories, wins, the sun always shines, and it never rains on our parade. Our self-image is built on externals. Things were going well, and Elijah said it was good to be alive. Enter Jezebel, and the prophet cried it is better to be dead.

Losing . . . Faith in Others

I suppose the next step in Elijah's despair was almost inevitable. When we lose faith in God and in ourselves, we usually lose faith in others. Elijah reminded God of how faithful he had been, and then he said, "I am the only one left, and now they are trying to kill me, too." It's lonely to be the only one left. We really do become isolated when we see ourselves as the only "spiritual person." Instead of others being fellow pilgrims, we set out to do life by ourselves. Everybody else becomes our competitor. Nobody else measures up. We live out of distrust.

Listening for the Whisper

What did God say to Elijah in the cave? When somebody is depressed, the instructions need to be simple. The message needs to be clear. "Go out and stand on the mountain in the presence of the Lord, for the Lord is about to pass by." How did God come? Not in the wind or the earthquake but in the "gentle whisper."

I suppose that when you have been to Mount Carmel as Elijah had, and you've seen God in the flash of the fire, it is easy to expect that God always comes that way. Not in the wind, however, but in the whisper, God speaks of divine presence. That really is the heart of the story. When Elijah felt most alone, the voice came to remind the prophet of a presence beyond himself. What Elijah could see with his eyes was not all there was. "Go out and stand on the mountain in the *presence of the Lord*."

That really is how God often makes God's self known. Look at Bethlehem. It's a whisper. God whispers, and Advent is the story of God's coming and God's presence with us. "You shall call his name Emmanuel," the angel said, which means "God with us."

Things do go wrong in our lives. Sometimes they go terribly wrong. Many of us know what it is to feel alone. Is there anything beyond us, or are we all by ourselves? The preacher rises on Sunday morning and looks into the faces of the listeners. Some have barely made it to the sanctuary. Life is overwhelming. On some Sundays, the preacher has barely made it. The minister looks out and then dares to say, "I want to speak today about the God who is here with us." It's quiet in the church house. No wind. No earthquake. No fire. People are listening for the "gentle whisper." If we listen carefully, we may hear God.

Chapter 5
The Last Word Is Peace

Jesus answered them, "Do you now believe? The hour is coming, indeed it has come, when you will be scattered, each one to his home, and you will leave me alone. Yet I am not alone because the Father is with me. I have said this to you, so that in me you may have peace. In the world you face persecution. But take courage; I have conquered the world." (John 16:31-33)

I'm not very good at saying goodbye. Some years ago when our daughter went away to college, I thought about what I would say to her when we had unpacked the car and the rest of the family was ready to go back home. It wasn't that Laura Beth was going away forever. But a child goes to college, and it's one of those moments when she walks through a door, and things are never just the same again.

For weeks I tried to plan those last words. The day came. We unloaded her things. My wife and I were standing in the parking lot ready to leave. The car door's open. I'm looking down, scuffling my feet in the loose asphalt. The time of departure is at hand. I look at my daughter. Last words: "Dad loves you, and I'm always here for you."

I'm sure you can do better than that. However, what I said is what I want her always to know. My love is unconditional, and I'm always available. She's married and lives now in Cambridge, Massachusetts. I would prefer that she didn't need me during the winter. If she did, though—rain, sleet, or snow—I'm on my way. "Dad loves you, and I'm always here for you."

These words of Jesus would be powerful spoken at any moment. However, according to John, these are the last words the pre-Easter Jesus spoke to his followers. He later offered a prayer to God; he said a few things to those who had arrested him; but according to the Gospel of John, this was Jesus' goodbye to his disciples. What do you say in a moment such as this? These followers were more than fearful. They were overwhelmed. The one who had been the center of their lives was leaving. Their pastor, preacher, and their Lord was leaving. This was no time for small talk. What do you say in a moment such as this?

In This World . . . Pain

Jesus begins by reminding them that the journey ahead will have pain. "In this world you will have trouble," he says. Jesus is not a preacher of a soft message that promises his followers only the high road. His is no message that ignores suffering. We would all like to hear that to follow Jesus means the bumps are removed, the curves are straightened out, and the road ahead is always smooth. That kind of preaching draws a crowd. If I can give people Jesus plus wealth, good health, and no failures, I can get a following.

The problem is it's not the message of Jesus. "In this world," Jesus says, "you will have pain." Sometimes that pain is public. We pick up the newspaper. Sarajevo. A few years ago this once beautiful city in old Yugoslavia was the idyllic setting for the Winter Olympics. Now people race to escape the sniper's bullets, and many don't escape. The city is in ruins. It's called ethnic cleansing.

The World Trade Center in New York City is bombed. A few minutes after 9:00 A.M., the Federal Building in Oklahoma City is destroyed, and among its victims little children in a day care center. In Charlotte, North Carolina, a young mother and wife visiting the city for the first time is killed by five young men who want her car.

Shall I go on? Violence permeates our society. The American Medical Association says that by the time a child leaves grade school, he or she has witnessed on the media 8,000 murders and 100,000 acts of violence. No wonder our children struggle with drugs and alcohol abuse. It's a way to deaden the pain, a bad way, but even for those of us who are adults, it's overwhelming.

Pornography? I'm for the First Amendment, but I'm not for something that turns women into objects and does violence to our personhood. Or the violence of words? I know a woman who will not return to church because she remembers a business meeting where people called each other names. She doesn't remember the issue that started it. What she does remember are the loud voices, the pointing fingers, and people poisoned by hate. This woman asked me, "If there's one place left in society where there is kindness, shouldn't it be the church?" She's deeply hurt. What do I tell her?

Do I remind her of Jesus' last words, "In this world you will have pain"? Do I tell her that the church is called into the world, but the world sometimes creeps into the church, and in the world of the church there is pain?

Public pain. It's around us. But there's also private pain—the kind that many of us have brought with us today—The disappointments, discouragements, the dashed dreams. Jesus could have made it even more personal, "In your world and my world there will be pain."

When our son was diagnosed with a brain tumor, it jarred the whole way I approach life. I like to plan things; I want to have control. Chaos and uncertainty are things I fear. We could do some things for David. We could try to find the best physicians and the best facilities, but then we had to wait for the tests and results, and the doctors themselves were not always sure of what was the best approach.

I suspect every Sunday in churches there are those who live with the pain of some uncertainty. Maybe, nobody else knows but you. Will my marriage make it? Will the job last? Will I ever graduate? Shall I go on? The list is endless.

Some years ago I walked into the room of a woman who was dying of cancer. "You are a minister," she said. "Yes." "You do represent God?" "I try." "God can heal the sick?" "I'm sure God can." "Well then," she said, "if you are a minister who represents a God who can heal people, I want you to pray that I will be healed." What do you say to that? I looked at her, "I will pray for God to heal you, but I can't promise that God will do that." She was disappointed with me. I'm sure she was thinking, "What good are you? I want to live. God is my best hope, and you are a minister, but you make no promises." Should I have reminded her that when Jesus was leaving, he said to his disciples, "In this world . . . pain"?

When I stood to preach each Sunday at Providence Baptist in Charlotte, I had a stained glass window with a cross behind me. The cross was empty. It reminded us that Christ was risen and there was hope. But it was still a cross, and it also reminded us that we did the worst of things to the best of God. Caligula, the cruel Roman emperor, said, "Crucifixion is educational." Maybe in ways Caligula never fathomed, he was right. The cross teaches us that in this world there is pain even for God. It reminds us that even the best people don't escape the battle.

In Christ . . . Peace

"In this world you will have pain," Jesus said. In the same breath, however, he reminded the disciples of something else: "In me you will have peace." The follower of Jesus lives in two dimensions: life in the world, life in Christ. It's not either/or; it's both/and.

In 1991 my mother died. I have watched my father as he's grieved. For almost fifty-four years they shared the thick and thin of life. When I visited him recently, I watched the sun fall across his face as he sat in his favorite chair. I could see the wrinkles, the age spots. When he walks now, he shuffles, a little unsteady. But I found myself smiling as I saw his face cast in the afternoon sun. I was remembering. When I was a child, the boys would gather in a group on the schoolyard and talk about whose dad was the biggest, the best, and the brightest.

My dad was. I was sure of it. It must be some macho thing with boys. I had never seen most of my friend's fathers, but I knew my dad must be the best. He always had the right answers. He walked me across busy streets when I was a little boy, and we always made it safely to the other side. My father was my security, my safety, and my superman.

But now I looked at a man nearly eighty-six, frail, memory not as sharp, asking me what I thought he should do about some things. I watched my father's face in the shadow of the fading afternoon sun, and I was reminded again that life changes, and often those changes are painful.

Jesus was leaving his disciples. The change was painful, the shadows of Gethsemane and Golgotha falling across Jesus' face.

Jesus was honest. "In this world you will have pain," he said. But then the twist—the other side, "In me you will have peace."

I watch my own father fade. It is a potent reminder of change. In a world of public and private pain, I need something or someone who is constant. That is the promise of Jesus. In me . . . peace. In Jesus we find the balance, the perspective, the power to live. In the Christ we find, as he said, the victory.

Goodbyes are not easy for me. It wasn't easy that day in the parking lot looking at my child. "I love you, and I'm always here for you." I hope my daughter knows how much I meant that. Things would change for her and for our family. One thing, however, would never change: I love her.

Jesus was saying goodbye. I hope those followers were listening. I hope you and I are listening. "In this world . . . pain." That's reality. We know it, don't we? There's another reality, though. I hope we know this too. These were his last words, "In me . . . peace." If we believe this, it will change our lives forever.

Chapter 6
Learning to Love Ourselves

When the Pharisees heard that he had silenced the Sadducees, they gathered together, and one of them, a lawyer, asked him a question to test him. He said to him, "Teacher, which commandment in the law is the greatest?" He said to him, "You shall love the Lord your God with all your heart, and with all your soul, and with all your mind. This is the greatest and first commandment. And a second is like it: 'You shall love your neighbor as yourself.' On these two commandments hang all the law and the prophets." (Matt 22:33-40)

In the midst of translating the New Testament, J. B. Phillips said the work of translation was like rewiring a house with the electricity still on. "You never know," Phillips observed, "when you will be shocked."

The problem is that for some of us the Bible has lost its shock. We have flattened out its message. We smooth out the rough edges, and we wind up with a Bible that fits the contours of our lives. No longer does the Bible probe, prod, or prick us. It simply sits there gathering dust.

The beginning of this particular story in Matthew is not especially shocking or surprising. The Pharisees raise a question with Jesus. Nothing unusual about that. The Pharisees were big on questions. "Teacher," one of them asks, "Which commandment in the law is the greatest?" The Jews were a people of laws. This Pharisee wanted to know what Jesus thought was the law at the top of the list.

It's here that the text takes a twist. Instead of one law, Jesus reaches back into the Old Testament books of Deuteronomy and Leviticus and blends two laws into one. Jesus replies, "Love the Lord God with all your heart, and with all your soul, and with all your mind. This is the greatest and first commandment. And a second is like it: 'Love your neighbor as yourself.' " What makes Jesus' response surprising isn't that he invented something new, but it's the confluence of these commandments. Love God, love neighbor, love yourself! This is not a multiple choice question where we choose one or two of the three. The only answer seems to be "all of the above."

Love . . . God

Few of us would argue with the "love God" part. Evelyn Underhill, the great mystic, once wrote, "We lift our eyes from the crowded bypass to the eternal hills." People of faith are called to live with the upward glance, to lift our eyes from the crowded ways of life to the transcendent. Those of us who preach assume that inside each human spirit there is the hunger for something holy, something different from what people may have yet found.

We talk about finding God, but we can probably talk more accurately about God's finding us. To love God with all ourselves assumes that God first loves us with all of God's self. The Bible begins with the announcement, "In the beginning God," and then the story that unravels is the story of a God in loving pursuit of a people. We find God, but God first finds us, and what we really do is respond to God's reaching to us. Nobody who heard Jesus that day would have been surprised to hear Jesus say, "Love the Lord God with all your heart and with all your soul and with all your mind." That's the bedrock of any faith.

Love . . . Neighbor

Probably nobody was shocked to hear Jesus speak about loving our neighbor. That seems the right thing to do, doesn't it? If we love the creator, we should love the creation. Of course, it would have been interesting to see how the Pharisees responded if Jesus had given his definition of neighbor. We know how inclusive Jesus was. Neighbors were not just folks who looked like us, talked like us, and thought like us. Neighbors were also people like the Samaritans.

We have all heard people say, "Well, religion for me is to do unto others as you would have them do unto you." The Golden Rule. Some folks think the Golden Rule is in the Bible. They don't know where it's found, but it sounds like something Jesus would say. Sort of like, "Love your neighbor as you love yourself." Make that statement in a crowd, and most people will nod their heads in affirmation.

The problem was Jesus had a big view of the neighborhood when he said "love your neighbor." Our own nation is racked by the violence of groups that spew hate toward those who don't think as they do. The world has witnessed a dangerous rise in rigid religions that seem to celebrate violence against others. We keep restricting the neighborhood to those who look like us, think like us, and believe like us. Jesus expanded the neighborhood. The marginalized of his day—Samaritans, women, lepers, Publicans—were to be loved not loathed.

"Love your neighbor," Jesus said. Who is our neighbor? What about those closest to us? Some have grown up in what we now call dysfunctional homes. She said to me as her pastor, "My father was an alcoholic and abused me." She was in pain. Children are good observers but poor interpreters. This woman trusted the big man in her house. He was her "daddy." But he abused her. She was in pain.

Some people walk out of domestic chaos everyday. You and I may never know it when we see them at the store, at work or even sitting next to us at church. They are in pain. At home the words fly—hurtful words, violent words. Jesus said, "Love your neighbor," and the fact of the matter is the neighbors hardest to love may be the ones we know the best.

Frederick Buechner tells the story of his father's suicide. One Saturday morning, Buechner and his brother were still in bed. They looked out the window to see their father lying in the driveway. They were just children, and their father was dead by his own hand. "For years," Buechner said "I couldn't bring myself to tell people how my father died. I would say he had heart trouble." Then, in that poignant way of his, Buechner said, "In a way I was right. My father did die of a troubled heart."

Jesus said, "Love your neighbor." Frankly, I have no trouble loving Samaritans or lepers. I haven't met any lately. But those close to us—living out the love of Christ with those who are closest to me? Now that's the challenge. The neighborhood widens; the neighborhood narrows. Jesus said, "Love your neighbor."

Love . . . Yourself

Jesus wasn't finished with the greatest commandment. He said one other thing. Sometimes this has been neglected: the little phrase, "as you love yourself." "Love your neighbor as you love yourself." As a child, I had a Sunday School teacher who impressed on the class the secret of "Christian joy." In fact, she used the letters in the word "joy" to make her point. "Jesus first," she said. "Others second; yourself last."

It certainly sounded spiritual to my young ears. Who could argue that Jesus should be first? Certainly we should be caring and compassionate toward others. Maybe my teacher intended that I would also love myself. I don't know. All I know is the word that stood out in my child's mind was "last." Last was last. In our pick-up ballgames, the person who was chosen last was not the most loved; he was usually the worst player.

One time when the comedian Woody Allen was interviewed, he said he had one great regret: that he wasn't born someone else. I have felt that way about my own self at times. Why wasn't I born with someone else's talents, gifts, abilities, or looks? I look back at my life, and I see a lot of hard work and achievement. I wish I could say that all I have done has been done with a sense of loving myself. Unfortunately, I think I have lived much of my life, as the country song says, "looking for love in all the wrong places."

Jesus said, "Love your neighbor as yourself." I suppose what Jesus was saying is that God made us, and whatever we are, we are God's. Trying to get the applause of the crowd is exhausting. Those of us who are ministers know the pain. There are days when we give the best we know how and wonder if anybody notices. Despite our best efforts, we will not be loved by everybody. On those days, can we believe that we are loved unconditionally by God? Can we love ourselves for who we are—children of God?

Not long ago I saw an intriguing bumper sticker. It didn't ask me to honk if I loved Jesus. There was no political agenda such as, "Don't blame me! I voted for _____!" This bumper sticker simply said, "Enjoy being." When I spotted it, I think I was running late on my way to do something. The message was, "Enjoy being."

I thought it might be good if we developed some kind of ceremony in the church where we had people stand in the front. "Do you receive yourself as the person God has made you to be? Do you promise to enjoy being because God has made you who you are?" What if everybody in the church said, "I do," and we all meant it?

"Jesus," his adversaries asked, "What is the greatest commandment?" It was a test for Jesus. Do you know what Jesus did? He made it a test for them . . . and for us. "Love the Lord your God with all your heart, and with all your soul, and with all your mind. This is the greatest and first commandment. And a second is like it, 'Love your neighbor as yourself.' " Do you and I pass the test?

Chapter 7
Do We Really Want to Be Changed?

We must no longer be children, tossed to and fro and blown about by every wind of doctrine, by people's trickery, by their craftiness in deceitful scheming. But speaking the truth in love, we must grow up in every way into him who is the head, into Christ, from whom the whole body, joined and knit together by every ligament with which it is equipped, as each part is working properly, promotes the body's growth in building itself up in love. (Eph 4:14-16)

Several years ago I was asked to perform a wedding. In the ceremony, I did my usual short homily. I spoke about leaving and cleaving. When the wedding was finished, I was waiting for the photographer to take the pictures. Several members of the wedding party came up to me. It became quickly apparent this wasn't a church-going group. "Reverend," they said. I don't like to be called "Reverend." "That was a nice talk you gave," they continued. I don't like to give "talks." They weren't finished. "That was a nice talk, but we didn't understand the word 'cleave.'"

Not only do I not like to be referred to as a "Reverend" who gives "talks," but also I don't liked to be questioned about my homilies. If you go to church, you know that you either get what the preacher says or you don't. I'm not used to having a contingent of people meet me and ask me about something they didn't understand.

However, this was a wedding, and I was feeling in an expansive mood. Besides, these were young people who hadn't been initiated into some of the antiquated vocabulary of the church and who didn't know any better than to ask. So I explained that cleave meant to hold onto something or someone. In life, I said, we leave or let go of certain things in order to take hold of something else. By this time the photographer was ready to take pictures, which was a good thing because I could tell that they were content with a one-sentence explanation and didn't want all that stuff about "life."

I want to use these words, *leave* and *cleave*, to speak about something important. Paul was writing to the church at Ephesus. It's apparent the church was experiencing some division. Paul speaks about the people being tossed back and forth, intrigued first by one doctrine and then the next. Like most first-century Christians, these people at Ephesus were susceptible to this type of thing. They didn't have the New Testament as we have it. Various preachers came through the city with their own "spin" on the faith. If some preacher sounded appealing, that preacher drew a following. These new Christians had little tradition by which to evaluate every new idea that came through town.

So Paul writes to them, and the Apostle basically says, "It's time to grow up." It's time to change. As painful as it may be to become different, the situation can't stay the same.

Leaving

Paul says that to change we need to "leave" some things. "We must no longer be children, tossed to and fro and blown about." The Apostle lets the church at Ephesus know that to "grow up" is to "grow out" of some things. One of the favorite services at churches where I have been pastor is the parent-child dedication service. The mothers and fathers come to the front of the sanctuary with their babies. I hold each child, read a verse of scripture, and have a prayer. It's a beautiful time. Sometimes I watch the faces of the congregation. People who never smile at me during the sermon are all smiles during the dedication service. The babies are beautiful. . . .

Except when they are in full cry at two in the morning. Or when they interrupt everyone else's schedule to keep their schedule. In fact, Augustine, the early church father who shaped so much of our theology, had his idea of original sin reinforced by his observation of children. Augustine said we come into this world wanting to be the center of attention and to have the world revolve around us. "We must no longer be children," Paul said. To grow up is to grow out of some things.

I recently spent some time on the campus of Princeton University in New Jersey. I love to see the T-shirts people wear in a college community. They make statements. One day I saw a man who looked like a leftover hippie from the 1960s with beads and sandals. He wore a T-shirt with the message, "Follow your bliss." I'm not exactly sure what that means. If it means we should be concerned about our own needs and what brings us a sense of satisfaction, I agree. But if "follow your bliss" means that we all fly solo doing our own thing without regard for others—if it means the primary purpose in life is my own happiness whatever that involves—I disagree. It sounds like infancy, self-centeredness, to me.

The latest theological notion whistled through Ephesus, and off went the crowd to follow it. Some charismatic preacher who had a twist on theology set up shop, and the shop was filled with Ephesians who became twisted in their own ideas. Ernest Campbell, former pastor of Riverside Church in New York City, lamented the loss of transcendence in our world. A secular society, Campbell said, is one that loses any sense of anything beyond itself. Campbell may have been right. He probably was. Maybe in the 1990s we are seeing a reaction to that void. People are flocking to all kinds of religious notions. For example, I go to the bookstore and am astounded by the large section on the New Age movement. I drive down the streets of my southern city, and it's not uncommon to see crystals dangling from rearview mirrors. People seem to be searching for something.

Witness the growth of sports and entertainment. If our heart and treasure are intertwined as Jesus said, then we have a serious issue. I like sports; I like to be entertained, but we pay millions of dollars to people who jump, shoot, pass, catch, sing, and dance. The passion in the stadium is more obvious than the passion in the sanctuary. What does all that say about what is central to our lives?

Several years ago my wife gave me a porcelain figure of a minister with his index finger pointed upward. Diane said, "The hand reminds me of you." What bothers me, though, is the minister's face. He looks harmless, almost irrelevant. Who wants to go hear him when I can go to the stadium and shout for my favorite team or go hear some slick-dressed preacher tell me that if I give his church a nickel, God will surely reward me with a dime.

Do you think another name for your town could be Ephesus? Or maybe my town? When my children were young, one of the worst times of the year was Christmas afternoon. By then they had gone through the gifts, and they were ready for something new. "How much longer to our birthdays?" they would ask. I tried to remember they were children. They were young. They liked the excitement of something new and different. I said to myself, "One day Laura Beth and David will grow up and grow out of this." They will learn to settle down. They won't "follow the bliss" if that means running "hither and yon" trying to find something novel. Laura Beth was home last Christmas. As we ate supper, I asked David and her if it had been a good day. "The best," they said. They didn't remind me about their birthdays. I felt good as a father.

Cleaving

There's the word that stopped the wedding party in its track—"cleaving." I can understand why. It's a wedding word. Do you ever use it in normal conversation? I don't. I can see my wife's face if I came home one afternoon and said, "Diane, I'm so glad I have you to cleave to!" "You've been reading that King James translation again," Diane would probably reply.

But today I want to recover "cleave." It means to hold onto. Paul says the Ephesians need to change. A part of that growing up is to grow out of some things. However, when we grow up we also grow into some things. Listen to the way the Apostle put it, "But speaking the truth in love, we must grow up in every way into him who is the head, into Christ."

The Ephesian letter is not the easiest Epistle to read. Its sentences in Greek are sometimes long and bulky. The letter contains some words and phrases that are not typically Pauline. Some scholars have questioned Paul's authorship. Let's assume for a moment that Paul did write the letter. Let's also admit that Paul's style at times in this and other writings is ponderous. Let's recognize that Paul didn't tell any parables or clever stories that always help us to remember.

Yet, these words in Ephesians are a memorable metaphor. The church is like a body. Christ is the head. The more we see that the body takes its direction from the head, the better the church will be.

However, if the arms and legs and every other part of the body is moving at its own impulse, the result is chaos. "Grow up," the Epistle says, "into him who is the head, into Christ."

What is true for the church is also true for us as persons. Anxiety literally means to be pulled apart, to be stretched from one thing to another. We have a lot of that in our time. We feel the push and pull of a multitude of demands. How do we find some kind of center to our lives? How do we give ourselves as Jesus said to the "one thing most needful" so that life has some balance? How do we grow out of the childish perspective on life that we can have it all and do it all? "Grow up," Paul says, "into him who is the head, into Christ." Jesus becomes the focus of our faith, the one thing most needful.

When our son David was young, he had a puzzle of Little Red Riding Hood. The puzzle had about fifteen big pieces. That's my kind of puzzle. I admire people who relax by putting together those puzzles with 1,000 or 2,000 pieces. That's not the way I relax. Fifteen big pieces is about my maximum. One night David and I put the puzzle together. When we had finished, we were missing one piece. We had fourteen out of fifteen, but one was missing. Guess which one it was? Little Red Riding Hood's head. We had everything but Red's head. We didn't look at it and say, "We still have most of the pieces. Fourteen of fifteen is a good percentage." No, we didn't say that. The head was missing. That's the only thing David and I noticed.

The Ephesians needed to change. Maybe you and I need to change. We go through life, and we leave some things behind. But there's something to which we need to cleave. Paul said, "Hold on to the head. Cleave to Christ." I know, "cleave" is a Saturday word, a wedding word. But if you'll let me, I want to make it a Sunday word, and really I want to make it a word for each day of our lives.

Chapter 8
The Power to Forgive

Pray then in this way: Our Father in heaven, hallowed be your name. Your kingdom come. Your will be done, on earth as it is in heaven. Give us this day our daily bread. And forgive us our debts, as we also have forgiven our debtors. And do not bring us to the time of trial, but rescue us from the evil one. For if you forgive others their trespasses, your heavenly Father will also forgive you; but if you do not forgive others, neither will your Father forgive your trespasses. (Matt 6:9-15)

What is the heart of the Christian faith? Is it right beliefs? Of course, doctrine is vital, but some would have us believe that as long as our minds affirm the "right" things, then we are right. Or is the heart of our faith right behavior? Jesus certainly told his followers that there were ethical standards for them to follow. Jesus called on his listeners to do as well as to believe.

Yet, I would contend that the heart of the Christian faith is right relationships. At least the Sermon on the Mount in the Gospel of Matthew seems to indicate this. How do we relate to the world? "You are the salt of the earth. . . . You are the light of the world." How do we relate to our spouse? "But I say to you that anyone who divorces his wife, except on the ground of unchastity, causes her to commit adultery; and whoever marries a divorced woman commits adultery." How do we relate to our enemies? "You have heard that it was said, 'You shall love your neighbor and hate your enemy.' But I say to you, Love your enemies and pray for those who persecute you."

Let's face it. These are hard words. For some of us who preach, our tendency is to try to tone them down. I have people in my congregation who have been through divorces. Maybe the reason wasn't "marital unfaithfulness." Maybe they divorced because of physical or emotional abuse. Maybe they tried everything they knew to do to make the marriage work. Am I to tell these people who are trying to put shattered lives back together that if they remarry it's adultery?

I confess I don't take Jesus' words on divorce literally. However, I do try to take them seriously. I do try to interpret them in the context of their time. Women were regarded generally as property, not persons. Men could easily get divorces. Jesus was taking marriage seriously and sacredly. Salt and light to the world, marriage, loving our enemies—all of these relationships are a part of the fabric of our lives.

But another relationship is even more central in the Sermon on the Mount. That is our relationship to God. Jesus begins the Sermon on the Mount with the beatitude, "Blessed are the poor in spirit, for theirs is the Kingdom of Heaven." Happy, Jesus says, is the person who realizes her need for God. Really joyful is the one who knows more than anything else that he is spiritually bankrupt and depends utterly on God. In the sermon, Jesus encourages us to ask, seek, and knock on the door of God. It's our invitation to intimacy, and as Helmut Thielicke has observed, the wonderful news is that God gives us a door on which we can knock.

In the middle of the sermon, Jesus offers his disciples a model prayer. Prayer is a powerful way by which we open ourselves to God. Jesus doesn't admonish or scold his followers, but he gently guides them into the things that move them from saying prayers to genuine praying. The Lord's Prayer is fairly simple—just fifty-seven words in the Greek. No long-winded, look-at-me stuff like the hypocrites on the street corner, but straightforward, simple, and short.

Forgiveness is among the areas that Jesus calls us to make a matter of prayer. "Give us this day our daily bread," Jesus teaches, and then he instructs, "And forgive us our debts, as we also have forgiven our debtors." On the surface nothing seems terribly strange about this request. Most religions teach people to forgive. When I go to a different church, and the Lord's Prayer is said, the main thing on my mind is whether I use "trespasses" or "debts." I was recently at a chapel service at Princeton Theological Seminary. The order of worship called for everyone to say together the Lord's Prayer. The order didn't specify "debts" or "trespasses." When the time came I said "trespasses." Everyone else said "debts." I felt I should ask for forgiveness.

Whatever word we use, however, the remarkable thing is that this petition expects something of us, which is different from the other petitions. Jesus didn't say, "Give us this day our daily bread even as we help to feed the hungry." Neither did Jesus say, "And lead us not into temptation as we assist others to avoid the traps." When it comes to forgiveness, though, there is an expectation of us as well as God. "Forgive us our debts," Jesus taught, and then the expectation of you and me, "as we also have forgiven our debtors."

God's Gift to Us

In a way, this petition models the journey of the Christian. The grace of God comes first. We turn to God in our need, and we ask for the gracious gift of God's forgiveness.

Of course, this petition presumes that we know we have need of forgiveness. Many of us grew up in churches where judgment was trumpeted from the pulpit and the sins were named. I knew the sins. I had a list of them: drinking, cursing, smoking, dancing—especially slow dancing, although square dancing seemed to be acceptable. As a young person, I kept the list close to my heart. In case I forgot, the pastor or some visiting evangelist was there to remind me. Don't get me wrong. There was some truth in what was said. Judgment is part of the gospel. Who needs grace if we are never guilty of anything?

Maybe what I rebelled against was not the idea that we all had failed God, but perhaps it was the preacher's harsh tone of voice or the idea that the list of sins seemed incomplete. Frankly, drinking and smoking are not major temptations for me. I don't dance very well, and since usually I have to preach an early service on Sundays, I have to be in bed early on Saturday nights anyway.

Whatever it was that I didn't like about that kind of preaching drove me to the other extreme. I liked to talk about the love of God. I was big on words such as grace, compassion, and acceptance. Then I recalled Dietrich Bonhoeffer's notion of "cheap grace." Who needs grace if you and I are never guilty? Can we preach the love of God and love for God without any call to be shaped in the image of Christ and to be more obedient to him?

Jesus seemed to think that you and I needed the gift of forgive-ness as much as we needed the gifts of bread and God's leadership from evil. Of course, deep down we know Jesus was absolutely right. Deep down we know we have our own list of sins. What about envy, jealousy, and worry? What about pride, prejudice, fear, and faithless-ness? What about injustice, inequality, gluttony, or greed? What about your own list and my list of all those things that seem to drive a wedge between God and us? What about those things that we have tried to overcome ourselves but still dog our days and nights? What about the sins that sap our strength and make us realize that what-ever else we become, we never stop being human.

I'm not much on extensive word studies, but isn't it interesting that the root of the word "forgive" is "give." Give as in gift; give as in grace; give as in the heart of God. Like every gift, it needs to be received. There's the rub. To receive is to be open. It's to confess that we need the gift.

God's Gift Through Us

The grace of God comes first. But Jesus isn't finished. "Forgive us our debts, as we also have forgiven our debtors." Some people have seen a problem here. Is God setting a condition on forgiveness? In other words, is God saying if you and I have love and forgive other people, then God will love and forgive us? Is this a self-imposed lim-itation of God where God says if we treat others well, then God will treat us well? If so, we come dangerously close to a theology that rests on human goodness rather than divine grace. Is this what we want? Do we want to walk out of the church building feeling that it's up to us to be compassionate and caring? Otherwise, God's compas-sion and care is nowhere to be found.

Or do these words of Jesus remind us that God is ready to for-give? The issue is this: Are our hearts ready to receive that forgiveness? Evagrius, the early church father, talked about the eight deadly thoughts. One of them was *acedia*, or boredom. It's when our faith becomes boring, the holy ceases to be sacred, and what seems vital to us is as stale as used chewing gum. The result of boredom is often envy and anger. Other people become our competitors, and forgiveness goes out the window with the rest of the sacred. We become like the elder son in Jesus' parable. We work hard. We go through the motions, but the meaning is gone. In those moments, even his own brother became the enemy of the older son. When we have those times in our lives, it is so hard to forgive. It is so difficult to receive. The gift is there. Anger, envy, or self-pity blind us to the gift.

Clarence Jordan used to say, "One meets the Father on one's way back from being reconciled with his brother." We might say, "You and I prepare our hearts to receive the love of God even as we forgive our sisters and brothers through the power of Christ."

Is this easy to do? Is it easy to forgive? For me it's not. I can hold grudges as well as the next person. I have a good memory. I remember the times I have felt slighted, ignored, or injured by some word or deed. It's not easy for me to forgive. That's why all the petitions of the Lord's Prayer are spoken to disciples, to people who live not out of themselves, but out of the power of Christ.

In case anybody missed how important forgiving is, this is the one petition that Jesus reemphasized. Immediately after the model prayer, Jesus said, "For if you forgive people when they sin against you, your heavenly Father will also forgive you. But if you do not forgive people their sins, your Father will not forgive your sins." Apparently, Jesus thought the power to forgive was central to the Christian life, and I suppose it is. We are not much good to ourselves, to others, and to God when we can't let go of some things. It's a painful way to live.

The next time somebody says, "Now what is it you Christians think is important?" I will tell her about my beliefs. I will probably say something about how Christ changes our behavior. Most of all, though, I will speak about how our God relates to us in Jesus Christ and how that gift from God makes all the difference. In my mind, that's the power that sets us free.

Chapter 9
A Faith to Meet Our Fears

*When evening came, his disciples went down to the sea,
got into a boat, and started across the sea for Caper-
naum. It was now dark, and Jesus had not come to
them. The sea became rought because a strong wind
was blowing. When they had rowed about three or four
miles, they saw Jesus walking on the sea and coming
near the boat, and they were terrified. But he said to
them, "It is I; do not be afraid." Then they wanted to
take him into the boat, and immediately the boat
reached the land toward which they were going. (John
6:16-21)*

Paul Tillich, one of the most influential theologians of our century, once commented on the nature of most sermons he had
heard. Tillich observed that there were three major movements
in these sermons. First, the world was in a terrible mess; second, the
world did not have the answers to the mess; third, Jesus was the
answer to the mess. Tillich didn't take issue with the truthfulness of
the statements. Rather, he was concerned about the order in most
sermons.

Why not present Christ as the answer at the beginning of the
sermon? Why wait until the end of the sermon when the preacher is
running out of time and the congregation out of energy to say the
main thing? Tillich argued that most people know the world is a
mess; most of the congregation knows they haven't found many
answers; and what people are hungry for is for the preacher to name
something that provides some substance.

That's not bad advice for those of us who preach. I can take you
to my sermon file and show you a multitude of messages that deal
with the mess. This form of preaching is popular with some people.

It's Eric Berne's game, "Ain't it awful," brought to the pulpit. We preachers talk about the mess in the world and how awful it is. The problem is little is said about any answers.

Maybe, that's one of the reasons why I'm drawn to the Bible. It's both "down to earth" and "up to God." The Bible points out the mess. At the same time it points to God. Take this story in the sixth chapter of John.

The disciples found themselves in the middle of the lake. The Jews were not people who liked wilderness or water. These disciples were Jewish. The Gospel of John says it was dark, and suddenly a storm swept across the water. Jesus was not with his followers. However, Jesus came toward the boat walking on the water. The Gospel says that the disciples saw Jesus approaching the boat, walking on the water, and the disciples were terrified.

Does this seem strange? According to John, what most terrified the disciples was the sight of Jesus. I know about the sermons that say it was night, and the disciples saw a ghost-like figure approaching and were afraid. But that's not what John says. The disciples recognized Jesus. They saw Him walking on the water, and they were afraid. Perhaps, a combination of things made the followers afraid. They were in a boat on water at night in the middle of a storm, and they looked up to see Jesus walking on the waves. There have been times when I have said, "I would like to see Jesus." If Jesus would just walk into my office someday and say, "Here I am. It's going to be all right." The fact is if that ever happened, I'd probably be headed out the side door. Think about your church service. Every Sunday I remind the congregation that the Christ is with us. What would happen, though, next Sunday if in the middle of the choir's anthem, Jesus came walking across the pews. I have a feeling we all would be looking for a side door to escape.

Whatever all the reasons, the fact is the disciples in the boat were afraid. They were in a mess. They needed some answer, some strength for the storm around them and within them. Jesus said, "It is I; don't be afraid." Could that be a word for us? It's a simple and straightforward word. But isn't that the kind of word we need when we feel overwhelmed? If I'm suffering, don't hand me a textbook. I don't have the energy to read it. If I'm terrified, I don't want a treatise. I can't concentrate. Jesus was simple. He told them who he was and what that could mean.

It Is I: Who Jesus Is

Jesus began, "It is I." In the Greek, it is even simpler. Jesus said, "*Ego eimi,*" which means, "I am." How we hear something greatly depends on the ears we have. If someone walked up to you or me and said, "I am," we would say, "You are what?" "I am" may be a complete sentence because it has a subject and a verb, but it sounds incomplete to my ears. To Jewish ears of the first century, however, it was complete, and it was powerful. God said to Moses in the Old Testament, I want you to leave Midian, go to Egypt, and tell Pharaoh to let my people go. "Who shall I say sent me," Moses asks. "Tell them, 'Yahweh sent you.' " Yahweh is a name that defies exact translation, but it means something like "I am who I am." "Moses, tell Pharaoh that 'I am' sent you."

Who is coming across the water to the disciples? Why it is the "I am." It is God! The Gospel of John is clear from the beginning who Jesus really is. The first words are, "In the beginning was the Word, and the Word was with God, and the Word was God. Once in awhile we catch a glimpse of Jesus' humanity. He cries when he hears his good friend, Lazarus, may be dead. But for the most part Jesus moves as the great "I am." He does what he wants, when he wants, how he wants. Jesus is controlled by nothing except his own sense of destiny.

Shakespeare's *Hamlet* begins with the words, "Who's there?" At night on the water in the middle of the storm, "Who's there?" The disciples recognized Jesus, but they may not have recognized that this Jesus was God. "Who's there?" Jesus said, "I am," and the Jewish ears of the disciples would have heard the echo of Yahweh.

Paul Tillich asked why we leave the good news that Christ is the answer to the end of the sermon. We know that the world is in a mess. We also know that we have tried to create our own meaning in the mess and have come up empty. There's no doubt the disciples were in a mess. They even had their solution. When Jesus came, they were paddling with all their effort to make shore. What Jesus offered was not a sermon on the storm; it wasn't a message about the mess. Rather, Jesus said, "I am," the gift of God's presence.

Fred Craddock tells the story of one of his most gifted preaching students. The young man graduated and was called to his first church. Eleven o'clock the first Sunday, and there is no preacher. The church sings, prays, takes the offering. Still no preacher. They have the benediction, and the young minister is finally located sitting on a bench in the town park. He's afraid. He has the gift to preach. He knows the awesome calling of preaching the presence of God to people. He's terrified.

The elders of the church sympathize, but they tell him, "Don't let it happen again!" The next Sunday the young minister preaches. That afternoon he writes his professor: "Dear Dr. Craddock, It's one o'clock Sunday afternoon. This morning I tossed a stone into the waters. Whether it created any ripples or the ripples reached the shore of anybody's life, I don't know."

This young minister was honest. Those of us who preach don't always know. Does what we say create any ripples, or do those ripples ever reach the shores of anybody's life? Often, we don't know. But we do know that a lot of people come to us in the nighttime of their lives. Storms are raging. We don't have all the answers. The best we can, however, we bear witness to the presence of God. Who's there? Jesus said, "I am," and that's the good news, the answer we need more than any other answer.

Don't Be Afraid

I don't want to overplay the order of the words Jesus spoke, but I believe they are important. He comes to the disciples as God. As God, Jesus is then able to say, "Don't be afraid." This one walking across the waves is stronger than the storm. He can say, "Don't be afraid."

In 1982, our family went to the World's Fair in Knoxville, Tennessee. My daughter wanted to ride the double Ferris wheel. "Dad, go with me," she said. I really didn't want to go. I don't like heights. But I didn't want her to know I was afraid. So I went. The time came when our compartment on the ferris wheel stopped at the top. We were swinging in the breeze. I was terrified. I closed my eyes. Laura Beth noticed. "Dad, you're scared, aren't you?" When we finally reached the ground, she announced to the rest of the family, "Dad was really afraid!" Everywhere we went that day she kept reminding me that I had been frightened. "Why don't you announce it over the public address system?" I said. "Let's let everybody know I couldn't handle it."

What was Laura Beth really learning? Our children come into the world, and for awhile dad can do everything. Dad seems strong enough for anything. Then they begin to learn. We dads are very human. Things go bump in the night, and we are afraid. Difficulties come, and we wonder if we can handle them. Laura Beth was right. On the top of that ferris wheel, I wasn't enjoying the view of East Tennessee. I was terrified. All I wanted was *terra firma*.

But Jesus is God, the "I am who I am." Even on the darkest night in the midst of the storm, he is able to say, "Don't be afraid." Did the storm disappear? Did the darkness immediately end? No. That's important to remember. As a pastor, I have so wanted to bring light and end the storm. A couple comes to see me, and their marriage is so fractured. As their pastor, I can't put it back together, and sometimes I feel useless. I go to the hospital and watch a young father die. Wouldn't it be wonderful to gather the family and say to them, "I'll bring an end to your storm." A few weeks later, I am in the church preaching his funeral and telling the family, "Yea though I walk through the valley of the shadow of death, I will fear no evil, for thou art with me."

The Gospel of John does not say Jesus stilled the storm. The miracle is he got into the boat with them and through the storm brought them to shore. That is our faith. Are we afraid? Sure we are. Are there storms? If you've lived any length of time, you know there are. The miracle is the "I am," the God to whom Jesus gave a face is with us. Faith in God brings us to the shore.

Paul Tillich was right. We preachers spend too much time talking about the mess. I want to know, and I believe you want to know, "Is there any answer?" Long ago it was dark. The storm was overwhelming. The disciples saw Jesus, and they were terrified. What Jesus said was simple. "It is I; don't be afraid." He climbed into their boat and brought them to shore. That was the miracle. It could be our miracle, our answer, right now.

Chapter 10
Is There Life after Divorce?

When Jesus had finished saying these things, he left Galilee and went to the region of Judea beyond the Jordan. Large crowds followed him, and he cured them there.

Some Pharisees came to him, and to test him they asked, "Is it lawful for a man to divorce his wife for any cause?" He answered, "Have you not read that the one who made them at the beginning, 'made them male and female,' and said, 'For this reason a man shall leave his father and mother and be joined to his wife, and the two shall become one flesh'? So they are no longer two, but one flesh. Therefore what God has joined together, let no one separate." They said to him, "Why then did Moses command us to give a certificate of dismissal and to divorce her?" He said to them, "It was because you were so hardhearted that Moses allowed you to divorce your wives, but from the beginning it was not so. And I say to you, whoever divorces his wife, except for unchastity, and marries another commits adultery." (Matt 19:1-9)

There was a time in the preaching of many of us when we made an assumption about families. It may have been a false assumption at the time, but some of us still made it. The assumption was that everybody in the congregation was part of a nuclear family. Mom, dad, children—all nestled in their quiet home. When we preached about families, that was our vision.

It may have been a false vision all along; it certainly is now. Those of us who are ministers stand to speak to a variety of family shapes. Some are nuclear families, but in many churches they are a minority. We preach to blended families, stepfamilies, single-parent families, couples who have decided not to have children, and single persons—some by choice and some by circumstance. I want to speak especially to some of you who are single by circumstance; those of you who are single because you have been through a divorce. Is there life after divorce?

Matthew says Jesus had moved from Galilee to Judea. Large crowds followed him. Among the crowd were the ever-present Pharisees. They had a question. Matthew reminds us that the motive of the Pharisees was to "test" Jesus. "Is it lawful," they asked, "for a man to divorce his wife for any cause?"

"Have you not read?" Jesus replied, and then Jesus took his adversaries back to the book of Genesis and to God's intention for marriage. Can you imagine how the Pharisees felt? They knew the Bible, and people who know the Bible hate to have the Bible thrown in their faces. "Have you not read?" Jesus said, and he held in front of them the ideal for marriage.

Ideal

The ideal is clear. Jesus says marriage is sacred. God's intention is for a man and woman to lock their lives together for life. According to Jesus in Matthew, the only grounds for divorce is "unchastity."

Recently, I taught the Sermon on the Mount. I was reminded again how difficult and demanding the Sermon on the Mount is. Jesus intensified the law. One of the issues he dealt with was divorce (Matt 5:31-32). Jesus said the same thing he said later in Matthew. Marriage is sacred. Moses allowed divorce because of the hardness of people's hearts in his time. But Jesus says the law is now intensified. A man may divorce, but only for "unchastity."

When I taught this study, I confessed my uneasiness to those who were there. I like to preach the tender side of Jesus. The Sermon on the Mount is filled with tough words. What do I do as a preacher and teacher? Do I preach it off the back of my heels? Do I wink and say, "Jesus really didn't mean this?" Do I try to explain it away and say, "Well at least Matthew allows divorce for 'unchastity.' Look at Mark and Luke. They allow no reason for divorce."

Or do I say, "Jesus is holding up the ideal whether you and I like it or not." Matthew seems to say that in Jesus the new era has come.

For certain, it's the era of grace, but not cheap grace. Jesus comes with acceptance, but he also comes with expectation. We are to love our enemies, do good to those who hate us, walk the second mile, and treat our marriages as divinely ordained. This is the ideal—what Jesus calls us to be. Are any of us all of this? No! Does this mean we are to twist the demands to fit the contours of our lives? Again the answer is no.

Reality

In reality, on any given Sunday I am preaching to some for whom divorce is reality. This is always the struggle of preaching. I lift up the ideal, but the fact is in so many ways I fall short of it. I can be as petty and peevish as anybody. I can hold grudges, say unkind things, and be as selfish as the next person. I preach the ideal to challenge myself as much as any of those who listen. The fact is I'm speaking to some people who once had a dream for a marriage, and that dream has been shattered. I want to speak about reality.

GRIEF

On many Saturdays I stand in a sanctuary, bride and groom in front of me: "Do you take Susan to be your wife . . . for better, for worse." "I do." It's a special time. Everybody's nervous. Everybody's excited. Suppose at the end of the ceremony, I leaned over to the couple and said, "This has been a beautiful wedding. You said the vows well; you've pledged your love, but let's face the facts: Your marriage has a 50-percent chance of not lasting."

I don't do that, but it is reality. In America today, half of the marriages will end in divorce. All of the wedding plans, all of the dreams . . . one day he walks in the door and says to her, "I want out." I'm sure some divorces are fairly painless. Husband and wife agree that divorce is the best thing. But the vast majority of divorces I have seen as a minister have been painful. People are confused; children struggle to make sense of it; somebody feels rejected; the dream has died.

We need to understand that dying comes in different ways. Each day in the newspaper there is the obituary column. People die physically. If they are members of a church, they usually receive ministry. People take food, write cards, the funeral is held, and the family is surrounded with love. What about our response to divorce? Something has died; something has been lost; it's a time of grief. What does the church do? Often we're confused. Sometimes we take sides and place blame. The fact is whatever the reasons behind the divorce, we usually have some people who are bleeding and who need our care.

Riding down the interstate several years ago, I saw a bumper sticker on the back of a camper: "Getting new wife. Need someone to take over payments on old one." It's amazing how close humor and hurt are. The man in the camper thought this was funny. A woman somewhere wasn't laughing. Look around the room the next time some speaker makes a joke about divorce. I guarantee you will find somebody's who's not laughing. A dream has died, and I have trouble myself laughing at the wreckage of dead dreams.

GUILT

Divorce is often perceived as failure. People bring expectations to marriage. Many of us grew up reading the fairy tales. Cinderella and the prince were married, and the last word we heard was, "They went off to the castle and lived happily ever after." Before marriage, Cinderella had problems. After marriage, life was bliss. We never get any word about disagreements, problems with children, midlife crises, or retirement issues. It's just "happily ever after."

Diane and I were married one week when we had our first argument. It was over some curtains in our small seminary apartment. I mean, after all, you may as well pick something "big" for your first disagreement. What I remember, though, is how devastated we both felt. We thought it was the end of the marriage. We imagined how our parents and friends would take the news. The wedding had been beautiful, and now a week later the marriage was "curtains."

We managed to make it through that "trial" and even a few others since then. What happened to the "happily ever after" part? A couple is married, and it's usually a beautiful time. They bring all their expectations. They leave for the honeymoon, and everyone is smiling. There goes a marriage made in heaven. Then the word comes—a phone call at the office—"Pastor, I wanted you to know before anyone else lets you know. Susan is back home. The marriage didn't work. Irreconcilable differences. John and she have filed for divorce. Susan feels she's let everybody down."

I've changed the name to protect the injured, but you've heard the story, haven't you? At the very time when Susan most needs God, the church, her family, what does she feel? Susan feels like a failure. That is painful. She expected the marriage to be wonderful. Everybody who knew John and Susan had great expectations. A knock on the door one night: "Mom and Dad, it's Susan; I'm home alone."

What do I say to people overwhelmed by guilt and shame? Do I remind them of Matthew 6:31-32 and 19:1-9? As a minister, do I say, "What happened to the ideal?" As a seminary student, I spent a summer in a clinical pastoral education unit. I was assigned as chaplain to the alcoholic unit. I went to the unit, told the secretary on the ward the times I would be available for appointments, and then I left. When I told my supervisor what I had done, I found out I had made a bad mistake. My supervisor was the confrontive type. "Those men on the unit," he said, "are suspicious of religious types. Most ministers have given them little but judgment in their lives. You go back and spend time with them, care for them, and maybe if you show a little compassion, somebody will let you be his minister."

The theologian Carl Michaelson said that when we walk into a room and speak the name of God, we rearrange that room. Michaelson's words and the piercing words of the C.P.E. supervisor have come to mean much to me. I'm a minister. I represent God to people. Some people—in fact many of us people—feel that we have failed God. I walk into a room, and, if the people know I'm a minister, it gets rearranged. Some folks want to tell me why they didn't go to church last Sunday; others want to know if I believe the church will be raptured before or after the tribulation; but some folks never make it over my way because to them I represent all the judgment of God, and they feel guilty enough. My supervisor said—well actually he shouted in my face—"You go back and spend time with them, and maybe if you show a little compassion, somebody will let you be his minister."

GRACE

God's unmerited favor. That was the definition that I always heard in church. It's a good definition except it misses the point that Jesus usually defined words in relationship to people. He touched lepers. Some folks were aghast. Others said it was interesting how the love of this man reached to everyone. Jesus never announced that the theme of any sermon was grace. He left the formal definitions to systematic theologians who followed him. Jesus simply treated everyone as a child of God, and later people called that grace.

It's the gift to see persons as persons and to let them know they are loved by God. It's the gift of moving beyond the color of someone's skin, the color of her ideas, or the color of his circumstances to see a person. Some people bear the label of "divorced." "He's been divorced, you know," and it's like a brand that gets burned into us and stays forever.

Several years ago I was walking through the neighborhood where we lived. A school bus pulled up and let off one child. I would guess he was about fourteen. I was close enough to see his face. I watched him as he shuffled to a nearby house. This child was physically and mentally challenged. For a moment I felt sorry for him. I felt sorry for parents who had dreamed of a healthy child.

I watched as he stumbled up the walkway to his house. A woman was waiting for him. I guess it was his mother. When he reached the front steps, she gathered him in her arms and hugged and kissed him. I had tears in my eyes. Who was this child? His circumstances were he was mentally and physically challenged. Who was this child? To his mother, he was a gift; he was her son. What do you call that? That afternoon I called it grace.

Who are you, and who am I? In one sense, we are all persons who have experienced pain. Most of us have had some great dreams that became nightmares. Some of you have been divorced. Is that all you are? Who are we? Whatever else we are, we are children. We are children whom the heavenly parent wants to embrace. What do you call it? I call it Grace.

Chapter 11
The Focus of Our Attention

After they were released, they went to their friends and
reported what the chief priests and the elders had said
to them. When they heard it, they raised their voices
together to God and said, "Sovereign Lord, who made
the heaven and the earth, the sea, and everything in
them, it is you who said by the Holy Spirit through our
ancestor David, your servant: 'Why did the Gentiles
rage, and the peoples imagine vain things? The kings of
the earth took their stand, and the rulers have gathered
together against the Lord and against his Messiah.' "
(Acts 4:23-26)

C. S. Lewis once said, "There are times in all of our lives when the angels hold their breath to see which way we will go." It was that kind of time for the early church in the book of Acts. The first three chapters picture a church where all is well. People are being converted; the church is growing; the fellowship is strong; in fact the comment is made that the church was "having the goodwill of all the people" (2:47b).

But the church's Camelot ends in chapter 4. Apparently frightened by the growth of this "Jesus" movement, the authorities arrest Peter and John. These two leaders of the church are hauled before the Sanhedrin, the Jewish high court. Peter and John are quizzed, threatened, imprisoned, and finally released. Undoubtedly, the authorities think intimidation is sufficient.

Upon their release, John and Peter return to the church. In the midst of troubling times, what does the church do? Where does it turn? On what does it focus its attention? I know times are different now. Few of us who preach face imprisonment. We may be ignored, but we are not in much danger of incarceration. Yet, there is a common issue. Where do we turn in the troubling times? What gets us through when Camelot becomes chaos, and the best of times becomes the worst of times?

The Look Around Us

Do we look around us to find the strength we need? Peter and John did come back "to their own people." All of us are debtors to others. Many of us have people who encourage us when we're afraid, bless us when we're burdened, and love us when we feel unlovely. Peter and John did come back to the community of faith.

Yet, the issue is whether anything around us, no matter what it is, can ever be the thing that ultimately sustains us. The community of faith is vital. I have been the pastor of churches, and every Sunday I have invited people to be a part of our family. But do we put our final faith in the church? Hardly! We know ourselves too well. We are the people of God, but we are people—frail, fragile, changing, getting some things right and getting other things wrong.

Several years ago when my wife and I were at a restaurant having dinner, at the table next to us was an older couple. I noticed she directed her husband to his chair. When the meal was served, the woman cut up his food and helped him eat. A younger man, who apparently knew them, stopped by the table. I was close enough to hear the older woman say to the younger man, "He doesn't understand much of what I say to him anymore."

When Diane and I got home that night, I couldn't get that couple off my mind. I imagined there had been other dinners for them—times when they had shared their lives and their love, and now that had changed. I admired the woman for the way she cared. That's hard when "he doesn't understand much of what I say to him anymore."

Look around. Things change. People change. I'm not trying to throw cold water on enthusiasm for life. So much around us is good, so much that blesses us; but there is so much that is broken. For the church in Acts, it had been the best of times. All was well. Suddenly, it all changed. The church was persecuted. It was the worst of times.

Hardly a week passes that those of us who are ministers don't meet change. Sometimes it is good. "Pastor, I have a better job." Or,

"I have met the man of my dreams." Sometimes it is bad. "I have no job." Or, "He left me, and the dream is dead."

Maybe that's why the church of Peter and John came together to pray. Maybe that's why the church began the prayer, "Sovereign Lord, who made the heaven and the earth, the sea, and everything in them." After all, when everything around us seems to be changing, we look for some constant. When life seems to be out of our control, we need to know a God who seems to have control.

The Look Within Us

When Peter and John returned to the church, they reported what had happened. Did these two apostles talk about their success before the Sanhedrin? They did have some success. There was a man who had been healed. "By what power or what name did you do this?" the authorities ask Peter and John. Peter answers, and his enemies are impressed with the courage of these disciples of the Nazarene. While they are "unschooled" and "ordinary," they make an impression. "They took note," Acts reports of the Sanhedrin, "that these men had been with Jesus."

Yet, when Peter and John report to the church, there's no sense of self-triumph. "Look what we did!" "Why, you would have been impressed with the strength we showed!" None of that! Rather, with the rest of the believers, Peter and John turn toward God. It's the move of dependence. No self-triumphalism here. The church bows its head and prays.

Several years ago I walked past a children's Sunday School class. They were singing. I stopped in the doorway to watch. "God is so high you can't get over Him; God is so wide you can't get around Him; God is so low you can't get under Him." I used to sing that song. The children loved it. When they talked about God so high, they stood on their toes and stretched their arms upward. God is so wide, and they reached out with their small arms. God is so low, and they squatted. It was fun, and it was good theology. I didn't interrupt their fun to talk theology, but what they were learning about God would be vital to their lives.

When I was a pastor, I would preach to some folks who had a lot going for them. They were intelligent, successful, attractive, and highly motivated. Many of them were gifted. There was the tendency to do life out of ourselves—to see God as an appendage. The problem wasn't Madelyn Murray O'Hair. I didn't preach into the teeth of seething agnostics and atheists. The problem was we believed God, but a God pushed to the margins as we tried to live out of ourselves.

I find this in my own self. I don't wake up in the morning and say as I'm brushing my teeth, "Now, do I believe in God today?" I assume God, which may be the heart of the problem. Frankly, I can go through whole days of being a minister with little thought of my own need for God. Little wonder there's so much fatigue and frustration in the ministry. God is somewhere, but where? We talk much about God but little with God. Who is God for me and you? That is the question.

Did you notice how Peter, John, and the church began their prayer? It is a prayer of faith and trust. It is more than belief in a God somewhere, somehow, some place. This is more than "to whom it may concern"; this is the "Sovereign Lord." This is the God who is "so high you can't get over Him; so wide you can't get around Him; so low you can't get under Him."

The Look Above Us

The prayer the church offered in Acts is short and simple. It has memory. The disciples remember the words of their forebear, David. In difficult days, many of us remember. We remember words of scripture that have strengthened us; we recall the faces of those whose faith has stretched us. In their troubling times, the early church looked back and remembered the God who had protected and provided.

The point is when their attention could have become focused on the problems, the community focused on God. I've called it the look above us. I'm aware we no longer live in a three-storied universe. I'm also aware that we speak of God behind us, in front of us, beside us, beneath us, in us, everywhere. The look above us is not an attempt to fix God in one sphere of space. Rather, it's a way of saying that the focus of our attention is God.

What amazes me about the prayer of Acts is the size of God that is portrayed. "Sovereign Lord," the church said, "you made the heaven and the earth, and the sea, and everything in them." When we face pain or encounter the unexpected, we often question God's size. Rabbi Harold Kushner wrote a bestselling book, *When Bad Things Happen to Good People*. Kushner faced the painful death of his fourteen-year-old son. When he wrote the book, Kushner said we have always spoken of God as all powerful and all loving. "I can no longer do that," the rabbi said. It's either one or the other. In a world where children die, you can't say both. Kushner concluded that God is all loving but not all powerful.

I know some people who face great difficulties, and it never seems to faze their faith. I'm not like that. In a motel room the night before our son's major surgery, I got down on my knees to pray, and I had no words. I wondered that night if I even had a God.

I've thought a lot about that night in 1983. Believe me, I don't want to spiritualize what was an enormously painful time. I felt deeply the absence of God. By no means was I a paragon of faith. But looking back, I think I learned something that night. I think I learned that when my faith is not big enough to hold God, maybe God's faithfulness is big enough to hold me. At least I made it through that night and each night since.

Could that be what the believers in Acts were doing? This is not a prayer about their great faith. In fact, no mention is made of them at all. This is a prayer about who God is and how God has provided. Really, it is a prayer about a God who is faithful.

The times when angels hold their breath to see which way we will go—the times when the sand shifts beneath our feet, and somehow we sense that life will never be the same. Where do we look in times like that? The book of Acts says in a time just like that, the church looked to God.

Chapter 12
Living with Wonder

*After these things God tested Abraham. He said to him,
"Abraham!" And he said, "Here I am." He said, "Take
your son, your only son Isaac, whom you love, and go
to the land of Moriah, and offer him there as a burnt
offering on one of the mountains that I shall show you."
So Abraham rose early in the morning, saddled his donkey, and took two of his young men and his son Isaac;
he cut the wood for the burnt offering, and set out and
went to the place in the distance that God had shown
him. On the third day Abraham looked up and saw the
place far away. Then Abraham said to his young men,
"Stay here with the donkey; the boy and I will go over
there; we will worship, and then we will come back to
you." (Gen 22:1-5)*

The Bible is usually portrayed as a book of answers. Sometimes,
however, the Bible raises disturbing questions. Take this passage
of scripture: "God tested Abraham." How did God test him?
"Take your son, your only son Isaac whom you love, and go to the
land of Moriah, and offer him there as a burnt offering on one of the
mountains that I shall show you."

This story raises some questions. Does that sound like the God
we've come to know and love? Or what about the voice of Isaac's
mother Sarah? Didn't she have anything to say about what was hap-
pening? The name "Isaac" means "laughter." He was the child of
promise born in the old age of his parents. They never expected to
have this child. Isaac was grace, but now God "tests" Abraham. The
story does end happily. Just as the father raised his knife to kill his
son, God intervened. A ram was sacrificed, and son and father came
off the mountain together.

This is not a story with easy answers. Walter Brueggeman says that in this episode we see how "serious" faith is. Our eyes are opened to the radical obedience of Abraham. Those of us who are preachers become poets trying to express something about faith but hardly able to explain the ways of God. The fact is here is a man encountered by God and asked to do something that seems barbaric.

Let's look at the story through the eyes of Abraham. In these verses Abraham says two things that give us insight into the way he saw and did life. He makes a response to the inbreak of God, and then as he starts the climb up the mountain, he speaks to his servants.

Here I Am: Wonder

God comes to Abraham and calls his name. "Here I am," the patriarch replies. "Here I am." On the surface these words seem little more than simple recognition—like the third grade class when the teacher calls the roll. "Abraham," God says. "Here."

But the Hebrew words drive deeper in their meaning. Abraham is saying, "God, I'm here; with all of who I am, I am present to all of who you are." It is what I would call, "living with wonder." In the midst of ordinary time, God speaks, and the old wandering Arimean springs to full attention.

Some of us remember when we first fell in love. I know it's different now. We talk to each other over the sound of the television, through the newspaper, and around the children. There was a time, though, when we listened with wonder. When Diane and I met, we talked about all kinds of things. Somebody passing by may have thought the conversation was silly. "It doesn't sound very important to me." That person didn't understand. We were in love, filled with wonder, listening to every syllable—the gift of presence.

Too bad we get distracted and often lose the wonder. Too bad we don't listen more as we rush off to the next urgent meeting or appointment. God said, "Abraham"; and with the deepest sense of wonder, Abraham responded, "Here I am."

Well, Abraham didn't have much else to do but to listen for God, did he? He didn't have the distractions you and I have today. That's the way I've often treated figures of the Bible. They were people sitting around with their hands cupped to their ears waiting for God to speak. But if we read Abraham's story, we will find he was busy. His son, Isaac, was growing. Time with Sarah. Abraham had made a treaty with Abimilech. He dug a well and called it Beersheba. Into the midst of this busyness, God says something, and Abraham is all ears.

I know as a minister how easy it is to get busy and lose any sense of wonder. The demands are heavy; the expectations are enormous. Like many of you, I say, "One day when life slows down, I will listen for God." The great fear I have always had as a minister is that I will come to the pulpit with nothing really to say because I have stopped listening for the voice from beyond. It's not that I won't say something. Most of us who are ministers have some gift for gab. But "gab" is hardly what you and I need when we come to the meeting place called church. We need to know that the sounds of the preacher have found some shape in the silent listening before God.

Abraham listens through the busyness, through the work, through the demands. He seems to live with a sense of wonder. His name is called by God, and he is fully present to the Great Presence of life.

Stay Here with the Donkey: Worship

"Take your son," God says, and Abraham does. Abraham and Isaac are ready to go up the mountain of sacrifice. Only father and son will make the journey. The servants will stay behind. Abraham speaks to the servants, "Stay here with the donkey; the boy and I will go over there; we will worship, and then we will come back to you."

One of the most startling things about Abraham's words to his servants is his description of what will happen on the mountain. He calls it "worship." As far as we know, there is no place of worship on the top of the mountain. Most churches have a place. They have an address, a phone number, even an answering machine. On Sundays, these churches have worship services. They print an order of worship, sing hymns, make announcements, and the choir sings. They take up an offering. Somebody preaches; the church prays; there's an invitation for decisions. Most churches call this "worship."

I'm not sure I would call what Abraham and Isaac were doing "worship." Would you? Yet, that's exactly the word Abraham uses. "We will worship." . . . No sanctuary, no sermon, no singing, and especially no offering! Abraham says what he's doing is worship.

It makes me stop to think about what worship really is. I mean, is what we do on Sundays worship? We come, we sit, we try to pay attention, and then we leave. What if somebody asked us this afternoon, "What did you do this morning?" "Why, I went to church." "What did you do at church?" "We worshiped." What does that mean? Abraham said, "We will go and worship."

It makes us wonder what worship is. Is it coming, sitting and listening? Is it a passive experience where the unordained watch the ordained do their thing? Frankly, I've been preaching for so long that it's sometimes difficult for me to sit in the pew. On vacation several years ago, I squirmed so much that Diane said I was a bad influence on our children. Ask me about worship, and I will probably tell you, "I'm getting ready for Sunday's sermon."

As far as we know, though, Abraham had no sermon. Yet, they went to worship. Literally, worship means "to bow down." It's to recognize something beyond ourselves that is so important that we say, "I'm all yours." The worth of God is so crucial that we bow before God with all that we are, including Isaac, the child of promise. Wonder is "I'm all ears." Worship is "I'm all yours, God."

Several years ago a friend asked me to preach a revival. It began on Sunday night. I arrived just before the service. It was a fairly small church filled with what I later found to be some of the most caring people whom I've ever met. I sat in the front looking at the congregation that first night. I noticed a young woman on the front row; she was in a wheelchair using a ventilator. Next to her an older woman—I assumed her mother. Before I preached, the choir sang a gospel song I had never heard. One of the lines of the song was, "We shall all be changed in the twinkling of an eye when Jesus comes." I watched the young woman in the wheel chair. When the choir sang those words, her mother put her hand on the daughter's arm. They looked at each other and smiled. The choir was singing, "We shall all be changed."

I was deeply moved. Driving home that night, I thought, "What was it about that scene that touched me?" Was it the picture of a young woman who would never dance, or jump, or even walk? Was it the mother? Those of us who are parents pray for the health of our children. The doctor says one day, "I'm sorry to have to tell you . . ." The mother places her hand on her daughter's arm, and they smile at each other. I know the pain for that mother must be enormous at times, but she has never stopped loving and caring. Or was I moved that night because here was a young woman in the worship service who knew she needed to be changed and one day would be changed?

Did I know that about myself? I walked into the service and walked out. I stood to preach, and I'm sure I said something about the difference Jesus could make if we would give him our lives. That night we had some prayers, sang, took up an offering, had the benediction; we called what we were doing worship. Was it?

A young woman and her mother on the front row—whatever they were, they were God's. They seemed to trust God. "We shall all be changed." These two people smiled. They seemed to believe those words.

Do you know what I believe? I believe worship took place on the front row of the church that night. I don't know whether worship happened in the pulpit. I don't know whether it happened in any of the other pews. But I believe it happened in the lives of two people who were saying, "God, whatever we are, we are yours."

Abraham and Isaac go up the mountain. What a tough story to preach! It should be. When we worship—I mean really worship—that's the most demanding thing we do. Abraham said to God, "I'm all ears; I'm all yours." Watch out if you say that. If you do, if I do, we will not be the same again.

Appendix
Preaching That Matters

I was fifteen years old when I felt called to preach. My home church pastor said that I should get as much experience as possible. Obviously, there was not a great demand for fifteen-year-old novices who were long on enthusiasm but short on skill. So, my pastor sent me to preach at a place that would take me—the rescue mission in Miami, Florida.

Each night the men flocked into the rescue mission. I wish I could tell you they were flocking to hear me. That wasn't the case! After the worship service, these men from the streets would be given something to eat and a place to sleep. They had to listen to the preacher in order to get the sandwich, soup, and a place to lay their heads.

I look back at those first stammering sermons with some embarrassment. I was far too cocky. I had no understanding of the world of my hearers. My dad would drive me in from the suburbs; I would deliver what were usually words of judgment; and then I would go back home feeling that God was surely pleased with me. If there is a special judgment for those of us who preach, I have a multitude of sermons for which I will need forgiveness.

The experiences that I had at the Miami Rescue Mission, however, have left an indelible impression on me. I will never forget them. One night, in particular, I remember it was the second time that I had ever preached. I had written carefully each word and had the full manuscript with me. Like most beginning ministers, I had one objective in mind: to get through the sermon without fainting, falling off the platform, or forgetting my place.

I was about five minutes into the sermon when a man on the front row raised his hand. I had no idea what to do. My pastor had not prepared me for such a time as this. In fact, to my knowledge I had never seen anybody in a congregation try to ask a question during the sermon. If you were a listener and you did not understand something, that was your problem. As far as I was concerned, the preaching event was strictly monological. The preacher spoke the words; the hearers kept quiet whether they understood or not.

But here I was at the Miami Rescue Mission with all of one sermon under my belt, and I had somebody with a question. I tried to ignore him. Maybe, if I kept preaching and raised my voice, he would get the hint. Unfortunately, he did not. The louder I became, the more he waved his hand. Finally, I stopped. He asked the question, and I gave some kind of answer.

For the life of me, I can't remember what the man asked or what I said. I think I was in shock. I remember the rest of the sermon was not very good. He had thrown me off my rhythm, and I was still stunned that anybody in the audience had the audacity to ask questions.

As professor of preaching at Baptist Theological Seminary at Richmond, I preach on Sundays in a variety of churches. The people in the sanctuary are polite and caring. They don't raise their hands when I preach. Once in awhile, I may get a puzzled expression on one of their faces, but they usually sit there and take it. Yet, I'm sure they have questions. We all have questions—questions about life, death, faith, love, hope, and the meaning of our days and night. We wonder about suffering and God's presence, about war, injustice and all kinds of ethical issues.

I preach with the vivid memory of the man in Miami who had a question and who suddenly turned my sermon into unexpected dialogue. Across the years, that man whose name I never knew has come to represent all the searching and questioning that are a part of many of us. We may not raise our hands, but we all bring to the sanctuary those longings to see things more clearly.

The chapters in this book are based on sermons that try to take seriously some of the questions people have and attempt to shed some biblical insight on them. In this sense, these pieces represent my whole approach to the event of proclamation. I have taught preaching; and for thirty-six years, I have been trying to do it. In the course of time, I have learned that there is a "grand mystery" to preaching. By this, I mean there is no program for powerful preaching, no one way to do it so that it is always done well. For sure, there are things we preachers can learn that will help us communicate more effectively. But the "grand mystery" is that God takes us "for better, for worse," and through the mystery of God's grace shapes the offering of our words into a word for people's lives.

With that said, however, these chapters reflect two things that are fundamental to my own preaching. First, sermons need to be connected to the lives of people. The congregation may not have their hands up on Sunday, but they do have questions. Eugene Lowry, who teaches homiletics at Saint Paul's Seminary in Kansas City, Missouri, would say they have an itch, and the preacher's task is to bring the scratch. My former teaching colleague, Raymond Bailey, used to remind his students that a sermon is a "particular word at a particular time to particular people." Good preaching is not a package that arrives at the post office addressed to everybody in general and to nobody in particular.

The reader will have to judge whether these sermons connect. If the truth be known, I may have had more people who wanted to raise their hands at the end than at the beginning. The reader will also have to judge whether there is too much attempt at relevance.

Frankly, I have learned to dislike the word "relevant." Sometimes we preachers try to squeeze relevance out of everything, and we wind up raiding the biblical texts and twisting them to our own purposes. This is the danger when the preacher begins the preparation of the sermon with the needs of people in mind and then moves to find the biblical text.

The sermons in this book begin with what I perceive to be human needs. For example, I'm convinced that things such as depression, anger, perfectionism, and grief are issues with which many of us battle. If we have done any reading in these areas, we as preachers also have insights into the psychological dynamics of something such as depression and perhaps even some of our own ideas about how to deal with it.

The tricky part is in the move to the biblical text. What if the Scripture does not say what we really would like to say? Who then assumes authority? Martin Luther said that the difference between Erasmus and him was that Erasmus sat over the Bible while Luther sat under it. Those of us who preach know how easy it is to try to sit over the Bible, and we either twist the text into an unrecognizable shape or simply read it and then leave it.

With that said, however, I do want to affirm the need for preaching that connects to the lives of the listeners. In 1991, I spent a semester on sabbatical at Candler School of Theology at Emory University in Atlanta, Georgia. During that time, I wrote a book on the subject of preaching. One of the finest parts of that experience was my work with Fred Craddock and having him critique each chapter of the book.

I will never forget the day that I went to see him after he had read the chapter on getting inside the lives of those who hear us. In his gentle way, Craddock pointed out that what I had written seemed to assume that everybody in the sanctuary was in the midst of some crisis. "Is it possible," Fred Craddock asked, "that some people could have had a good week, have their lives pretty well together, and have come to church to celebrate the goodness of God?"

Of course, Craddock was right. Not everybody in the church has a crisis, and not everyone in the sanctuary is suffering or has had a major setback. Yet, I would contend that in all of our lives there is the need to discover more of how the gospel can become our "good news." People come to the church house not just to hear what the Bible says, but to try to hear what the Bible says to them in the living of their days and nights. Therefore, one of my fundamental convictions about preaching is that it needs to be related to the lives of people.

The second thing I hope readers notice is that I believe deeply sermons need to find their authority in the biblical text. I have a high view of the Bible. I refrain from words such as inerrancy and infallibility because they always mean what the user wants them to mean and because they are really not big enough anyway. The test of biblical preaching is not some minister's saying what he or she believes about the Bible. Rather, it is assuming the power of the Bible to bring us to know the God of Christ and trying to turn that power loose to have its way among us.

In attempting to do that, three elements have become important in my own definition of biblical preaching. First, the preacher must give attention to the biblical text or texts that are used. I prefer to read the Scripture passage just prior to the sermon. In my mind, the reading of the text represents a promise that the sermon will deal with that part of the canon. Frequently, I will begin a sermon with the text itself. My assumption is that the Bible rightly proclaimed and heard generates its own interest.

I do not assume that the Bible is inherently boring, and thus preachers need to get attention with some clever introduction before they move to the text. Even in sermons where I do not begin with the text, I try to move there as quickly as possible and then attempt to weave that text throughout the entire sermon. For me, this is the heart and soul of biblical preaching. Those of us who preach take most seriously the text and ask not only what it meant but also what it means to us now.

A part of what has moved me in this direction is the growing conviction that many folks do not know the great themes and stories of the Bible. This is true even for those of us who preach in America's Bible Belt. Assuming that we can read a passage of Scripture and then simply "squeeze the juice" because everybody already knows the contours of the text is a false assumption. Sermons do need some teaching component to them. Obviously, this should not be so heavy that we lose our listeners in an avalanche of details.

Good African-American preaching models for us the effective use of the biblical text. The stories are told with enthusiasm. The preacher assumes the power of the Bible. The congregation hears how God has liberated the people in the past, but they also hear that God wants to liberate us in the present and to free us to face the future.

In addition to attention to the biblical text, those of us who preach need to hear the text in the context of its literary genre and the particular place where it falls in the canon of the Scripture. For example, the ninth chapter of John is a fascinating passage. It begins with a sightless man who is healed by Jesus. This precipitates intense discussion about who Jesus is. The Pharisees, the formerly sightless man's parents, and even the man himself try to figure out who this Jesus of Nazareth really is. Is Jesus the Son of God, or is he some slick charlatan? Is Jesus saint or sinner?

This is one of the central themes of John's Gospel: Who is Jesus? He marches onto the stage of the fourth Gospel as the Son of God; as John puts it, "In the beginning was the Word, and the Word was with God, and the Word *was* God." The Gospel is out to make this point, and Jesus is trying to open people's eyes to who he really is. Jesus is divine. Jesus is God, and throughout the fourth Gospel, he moves as "one with authority."

The last part of the ninth chapter focuses the issue for us. What Jesus is really dealing with spiritual blindness. The Pharisees ask him, "What? Are we blind too?" And, of course, the answer is yes. They are blind to who this Jesus is and what he wants to become to them.

A good preacher does not see the Bible as just a collection of sixty-six books. The Bible is more like an anthology. It sings, it chronicles, it tells stories. The Bible comes as letters, apocalypse, poetry, hymns, genealogy, and in a multitude of other forms. To know this and to keep it in mind enriches our proclamation and helps our congregations to know the many splendored dimensions of the Bible.

A third element essential to biblical preaching is that the individual text is always interpreted in light of the biblical message as a whole. Entire denominations have grown up around the interpretation of some particular passage. Come to Richmond, Virginia, and I will show you churches of all denominational stripes that claim they believe and preach the Bible. The people in these groups will even show you biblical passages to support their claims.

The fact is none of us preaches "pure Bible." We all have our angles of vision, our methods of interpretation. When I was a teenager, I remember a striking young evangelist who came to our church. He was the master of the clever cliché. His favorite phrase was, "The Bible says it; I believe it; and that settles it." I said, "Amen." It sounded good to me. I certainly wanted to believe the Bible.

The problem with the clever cliché is that it tends to reduce things and in the process sometimes distorts the very truth it seeks to proclaim. What the evangelist did not mention is what he was doing himself as he preached and what we all do with the Bible. We interpret it. We say what we believe it means.

Included in these pages is a sermon on divorce. I chose Matthew 19:1-9 as the text, but I immediately had a problem. Matthew 19:9 reads, "And I say to you, whoever divorces his wife, except for unchastity, and marries another commits adultery." That seems clear enough except when you compare Matthew to Mark's and Luke's account of what Jesus said. Both Mark and Luke say that anyone who divorces for whatever reason and then remarries commits adultery (Mark 10:11; Luke 16:18).

What do we do? Somehow we have to interpret these differences by whatever principles of interpretation we may choose. In the sermon I preached on Matthew, I exercised two principles. First, I tried to see Matthew as the unique Gospel it is. My purpose was not to try to harmonize the accounts. Rather, it was to see the Matthean community as it remembered the words of its Lord. And then I tried to apply them to the situation it was facing. Could it be that as the church grew it began to embrace more people who had been divorced? While trying to preserve the strong affirmation of marriage Jesus made, this community of faith wanted to provide some possibility for persons who had been divorced to have again the opportunity to marry.

My second principle of interpretation is that the specific always needs to be interpreted in light of the whole. In other words, a certain text needs to be understood in the light of what we perceive to be the thrust of the whole Bible. Entire religious groups have pitched their tents around a particular passage of Scripture they have interpreted in a certain way. These groups would claim to be biblically based. Many of them would argue that they believe deeply in the inerrant, infallible Bible. Again, the issue is one of how we interpret something in the Bible.

What about the whole sweep of the Bible? After everything has been read about Jesus, what is the portrait that emerges? Certainly, there is judgment in much of what Jesus says. He is not the pale Galilean proclaiming a gospel of cheap grace. Jesus' invitation to follow him is direct and demanding. He does not invite us to do our own thing and then bless it in his name.

Yet, when we look at the full stretch of Jesus' ministry, we are impressed with the gospel of amazing grace. People who seem beyond forgiveness are forgiven. Folks who are forgotten are noticed and become the honored guests at the great banquet. Those whose lives seem shattered beyond repair are welcomed home and are given a ring, a robe, and shoes for their feet.

The good news of the Galilean is that you and I always have another chance with him. Thus, when I preach on a tough issue such as divorce, I know there are people listening who wonder if they can remarry. While I want them and all who listen to know that it is God's intention for people to remain together in marriage, I also want them to understand that not a single one of us in the sanctuary has not known disappointment in some way.

I hope the reader of this book senses that I have tried to take the biblical text most seriously. In my mind, preaching is not preaching unless the trembling words of the preacher are connected to the Word that God spoke and continues to speak to us.

As I write these words, I'm in the western part of North Carolina sitting at a table in a house that overlooks a beautiful range of mountains. I cannot help but think about the first so-called mountain I ever saw. Growing up in Miami, the geography was flat. But I do recall in one section of the city, there was a hill. Actually, I believe it was just a little rise in the road. On some Sunday afternoons, our family would drive out to see this "mountain." In fact, this is what many people did on Sunday afternoons. Then, one summer our family took a vacation to the real mountains. Suddenly that little rise in the road didn't seem like much, and I don't think we ever went there again.

When I preach, I would like for people to see the Bible as the splendid mountain it is. Why argue about the mountain? Why try to find the exact words to describe its magnificence? Why not behold it and then try to share something of its grandeur? That is the high calling of preaching. It is always more than any of us can do, but it is a high and holy calling. The folks sit in the sanctuary on Sunday. They may not have their hands raised, but they do have their questions and their needs. The preacher opens the Bible and begins to speak. Who knows what God may do in that sacred hour?